D1545057

The ability to manage

The ability to manage

A study of British management, 1890–1990

S. P. Keeble

Manchester University Press
Manchester and New York
Distributed exclusively in the USA and Canada by St. Martin's Press

Copyright © S. P. Keeble 1992

Published by Manchester University Press
Oxford Road, Manchester M13 9PL, UK
and Room 400, 175 Fifth Avenue, New York, NY 10010, USA

Distributed exclusively in the USA and Canada
by St. Martin's Press, Inc.,
175 Fifth Avenue, New York, NY 10010, USA

British Library Cataloguing–in–Publication Data
A catalogue record for this book is available from the British Library

Library of Congress Cataloging–in–Publication Data
    The ability to manage: a study of British management, 1890–1990/
Shirley Keeble.
    p.   cm.
Includes bibliographical references and index.
ISBN 0-7190-3423-X
    1. Industrial management–Great Britain–History.   2. Industrial
management–History.   I. Title.
HD70.G7K43   1992
658'.00941—dc20   91–44098

ISBN 0 7190 3423 X *hardback*

Printed in Great Britain
by Bookcraft (Bath) Limited

Contents

Acknowledgements

The title of this book – *The ability to manage* – makes no claim to originality. It follows *The Power to Manage* by Eric Wigham, and *The Right to Manage* by Howell John Harris, and to both authors I acknowledge my debt.

Other acknowledgements and thanks are due. Most of the bodies which I approached for access to their archives gave their permission, and I wish to record my thanks to these companies, professional associations, and universities. They are all listed on pp. 164–5, together with brief details of each of the collections used. I am also very grateful to my colleagues Howard Gospel, Terry Gourvish, and Geoffrey Jones for their detailed and helpful criticisms of earlier drafts; to the Business History Unit at the London School of Economics for institutional support, and to the Economic and Social Research Council for funding the work.

S.P.K.

Chapter 1

Introduction and background

An accusing finger has been pointed almost permanently at British leaders of industry and their aides since Britain's industrialisation first got under way. When in the mid-nineteenth century Britain became the workshop of the world, industrialists were Satans throwing up dark forbidding mills and dingy workshops: from the late nineteenth century, as Britain has moved further and further down the list of major industrial powers, industrialists have been incompetents. Satans are normally beyond rehabilitation by modern historians; but mere incompetents in positions of power are, quite rightly, very suitable subjects for further study and possible reassessment.

Late Victorian and Edwardian businessmen – some incompetent, some not – have attracted a great deal of attention from economic historians in recent years in the great debate on possible 'entrepreneurial failure' in the late nineteenth century. Their successors have not been neglected in the continuing debate on the reasons for Britain's comparatively poor economic performance in the twentieth century. Much of the assessment has remained critical, although of varying intensity. It ranges from the acknowledgement of a 'general slowness to embrace change' over the past century,[1] to the identification of a long-running failure by British businessmen to make crucial investments in manufacturing, marketing, and management capabilities.[2] When the spotlight of investigation has been turned directly on to British businessmen, it has rarely failed to highlight their low levels of education and training when compared both to the levels enjoyed by their more successful foreign counterparts and to the requirements of industry. Why education and training levels have remained low, particularly in the period

1

since the Second World War when 'the "traditional weaknesses" in education and training, in company financed research and development, and industrial relations, have mattered rather more in the economic environment...and have thus had a significant impact on relative decline',[3] is addressed in the following chapters.

The book is concerned with the business practices and policies which have produced Britain's much criticised owner-managers and managers since the 1890s, and the efforts which have been made, and are being made, to reform the British approach to management formation to accord more with the needs of a major twentieth-century economy. It identifies a century of weak demand from business for managers qualified by education and wide experience, and discusses possible future directions to stimulate demand.

The work falls into two parts. The first part, which covers the period from the 1890s to the 1960s, traces the origins and development of the systems to produce corporate managers used in Germany, Japan, the United States, and then Britain. It chronicles a number of initiatives which offered British business a radical alternative to the *ad hoc* practices which constituted the British way. This alternative was a 'professional' training, in the sense that it combined a relevant higher education with practical experience. It was not intended, however, to lead to membership of a professional body: there was no role for a professional qualifying association. The second part, from the 1960s to 1990, emphasises the British employers' continued preference for the British individualistic approach, rather than for a more structured system with clear stepping-stones from the education system into a managerial career.

It is clear that at the beginning of these two periods, that is, in the decades of the 1890s and the 1960s, British business was presented with both the need and the opportunity to make marked changes to the ways it produced its managers. The need for radical change arose from the concurrence of a number of economic and technological phenomena which demanded a strong entrepreneurial response from businessmen. In the 1890s the need for change arose, first of all, from the fact of rapid industrialisation abroad and the growing competitiveness of other economies, notably Germany and the United States. Britain's economic performance and industrial structure were not such that 'business as usual' would adequately meet this competition. Its pre-eminence could no longer be taken for granted. While recent work on national income figures indicates that the UK in the 1890s did not, in fact, experience a break in trend or climacteric in economic growth,[4] they continue to point to fairly low rates of long-term growth. The period 1874–89 saw a rate of growth of 1.6 per cent per annum, followed by 2.2 per cent per annum for 1889–99, and 1.5 per cent for 1899–1913. Multi-factor productivity growth (a measure of ouput per unit of total input, allowing for capital, land, *and* labour) was less than one per cent per annum throughout the nineteenth century.[5] Moreover, the high British share of world exports of manufactures was based to a very large extent on textile and third-world markets: Britain's comparative advantage lay in commodities intensive in the use of capital and unskilled labour, while other economies had a comparative advantage in skilled labour (human capital)-intensive goods.[6]

There was, too, in the late nineteenth century, the fact of the Second Industrial Revolution. The educated, the inventive, and the entrepreneurial in this country and abroad were now taking each industry forward more rapidly with improved technologies, and they were developing sophisticated, science-based industries (primarily organic chemicals, electricals, and advanced mechanical construction). Their dynamism produced not only more advanced products and processes, but the business systems and production methods which were needed to produce them competitively. The Second Industrial Revolution brought with it the potential for major business successes, and the potential for large penalties to those who made the wrong choices.

Yet British businessmen were already displaying a propensity to move only slowly towards the new, whether that new applied to machinery, business methods, or products and processes. Textiles and cotton stayed for long with old machinery; steel with the more expensive Bessemer converter; engineering with unimpressive selling methods; alkali manufacture with the less efficient Leblanc process. Coalmining moved only slowly towards mechanisation; shipbuilding towards pneumatic riveting tools; building towards steel-framed construction. Many of the products and industries which were doing well had required for entry only simple technologies and a business head which understood local markets (like soaps, paints and pills, chocolate and confectionery, tobacco and brewing products). These then expanded by exploiting the cost advantages of scale. It has been noted that British industrial fortunes before the First World War came from these branded, packaged products, and not from oil, industrial chemicals, and metals, as they did in the United States and Germany.[7] Britain, indeed, never took the lead, either in production or in exports, in the principal 'new' industries of the Second Industrial Revolution.[8] Its performance in chemicals was particularly disappointing. The British had progressed rapidly until the 1860s. Technical progress thereafter held out the possibility of chemicals becoming a leading sector, but British entrepreneurs were unwilling or unable to make the shift to capital-using and resource-saving investment and innovation.[9]

There was, in addition, in the 1880s and 1890s the emergence of the modern, manufacturing, multinational enterprise, with its attendant difficulties of control over great distances. British companies, it has been shown, were very active in establishing manufacturing subsidiaries overseas.[10] At the same time, there was, particularly in the 1890s, a great increase in merger activity, which added to the need for managements of high competence.

In these more challenging business conditions, there was pressure on businessmen to begin demanding higher standards of education and experience of their successors. The pressure came not only from the perceived need that businessmen themselves acknowledged, but also from the many critics of business performance, in government, business, the press, and in education. It had long been clear that Britain was being challenged with increasing effectiveness by foreign competitors and that many business practices in British firms were in need of reform. A strong theme running through the criticisms was the fact of the better education and training of young foreign men in business, and the second fact of British education's willingness to increase its efforts for the young in the UK.

Britain around the turn of the century was tackling with some vigour the results of decades of uncoordinated and fairly minimal efforts which constituted the nation's education system. It was a time when education at all levels was the subject of much heated debate, and a strong lobby emerged to argue for a greater part of education to be focused more directly on the world of work. In the general expansion of educational provision, numerous small initiatives were begun throughout the country in vocational and technical education, and they looked to employers to help them grow. The technical schools and colleges offered to help raise the educational standards of semi-skilled and skilled manpower in workshops and offices, while the new university colleges hoped to attract men who aspired to a degree or to membership of a professional institute. The colleges also began to offer specially constructed courses to those looking for a career in large business organisations. British businessmen were presented with the opportunity, through education's need to co-operate to attract funds and students, to profoundly influence this development. They could help it grow, and influence it strongly in the direction of the needs of industry, or they could starve it of support and watch it wither.

A concurrence of similar phenomena in the 1960s made this decade a second period of need and opportunity. As in the 1890s, Britain had just emerged from a long period when the level of competition in world markets had not been high. From the early 1930s and well into the 1950s competition had been dulled by tariffs and collusive agreements, as well as by the needs of war and the post-war sellers' market. By the 1960s Britain was again exposed to strong competitive forces in an open international economy. It was a period of rapid technological change, and of high merger activity. A marked increase occurred in the scale and scope of the largest manufacturing organisations. And, as in the 1890s, the level of response from British business to the more challenging conditions which now prevailed caused increasing concern. Britain's economic performance was still good compared to its own historical effort, but its sharp decline in the international league tables showed that a much higher level of achievement was called for. Critics noted, as their predecessors had done, the better education and training of foreign business managers, and, very pertinently, education's continued willingness to respond to strong signals from students and employers. It was hoped, again, that the great expansion of the education system would allow industry to make its demands, and that the strength of the demands would allow education to respond, to the benefit of both.

However, neither industry's need to provide itself with a more effective system of producing its corporate managers, which the conditions of the 1890s and 1960s highlighted, nor the opportunity which the great expansion of educational facilities in these decades offered, was sufficient to persuade many businessmen to act. There was no marked shift away from existing practices, which leaned heavily on chance to produce the right men, towards a pattern which was more certain of producing men who were efficient by international, not merely British, standards.

The rest of this chapter begins to analyse why management policies on the production of new managers have proved to be so resistant to major reform over much of British industry and for such a long period. It looks at a number of restraints to change, the first of which can be looked at in terms of 'over-commitment'.

The generations of businessmen who had lived through the years of the First Industrial Revolution left a heavy burden of heritage to their successors. Firstly, they had produced what was seen as a winning formula for business success. This combined a strong reliance on market forces and an empirical approach to technological advance with the innate capabilities of the British businessman himself. Their immediate successors were faced with the choice of fundamentally altering what had recently helped to make British firms prosperous or continuing to make small changes as and when they seemed necessary. Later generations were faced with making radical changes to practices which were now part of the fabric of business life. Resistance to radical change is not peculiar to British businessmen, and is not important where the winning formula remains a winning formula from one generation to the next. In Britain's case, however, the winning formula was proving to be in need of some amendment even before the 1890s.

The burden of heritage also included the very strong impact which these earlier generations made on their successors and their firms. The impact was made by businessmen who had largely shaped the First Industrial Revolution, but who themselves had been largely shaped by it. For 100 years Britain had spawned good numbers of men prepared to respond to the abundance of manpower and materials, to the manufacturing techniques coming into existence, and to the opportunities in foreign trade and financial services. Britain had produced businessmen of high reputation in all the major industries – in coal, iron, textiles, mechanical engineering, railways, and shipbuilding – by the mid-nineteenth century. The names of British manufacturers sat proudly on goods which gave excellent service throughout the Empire. In 1870 they accounted for nearly one-third of the world's manufacturing production, still far ahead of the output of the United States. But the markets had been large enough world-wide and the products of most industries unsophisticated enough to allow comparatively easy entry, and entrepreneurship was largely imitative, not innovative. Change came slowly over many decades. For the mass of British businessmen, therefore, there had been no great requirement to possess outstanding technological skills, innovatory capabilities, or large financial resources. A stronger characteristic was their individualism.

Myriads of small firms had emerged in the nineteenth century, headed by myriads of independent-minded owner/managers. A few firms, especially capital intensive firms, had begun as large ventures or grew large; but many small firms continued in existence – often on the edges of survival, as trade cycles battered them with distressing frequency. The experiences of the participants in this First Industrial Revolution, and the prevailing political attitudes, which supported 'setting individuals free to pursue their own interests and to make what use they wished of their own property, without reference or interference from the state',[11] had encouraged in them a sturdy and stubborn individualism.[12] But the powerful currents of individualism in British businessmen soon showed that they could pull strongly in the wrong direction. When, in the late nineteenth century, foreign competition made business conditions much harder and the levels of technological skill required to enter modern industries were rising sharply, many British firms were hard pressed to remain at the forefront of change in their industry, or to catch up after they had been overtaken. They had in the past followed the innovators; but now the innovators were moving into areas too far removed from everyday understanding or too radical to be contemplated, too far outside the boundaries of the capital, the technology, and the markets that were reasonably accessible to them. They responded by making adjustments to their existing practices, when the risks attached to the change seemed very manageable. Slow incremental change within the resources of the individual firm had brought success in the past and most British manufacturers saw this as the only policy for the future. Businessmen and firms did join groups, but these tended to have the main aim of protecting a threatened interest rather than that of collaboration and mutual assistance.

Individualism in an entrepreneur is advantageous to success: it prompts him to take those important first business decisions and leads where others would never have thought to tread. But the narrowly individualistic have limited horizons. They refuse to tap the full resources of others whether inside or outside the firm, and they cling to personal power even when it stands in the way of the firm's advancement. The most successful economies rejected narrow individualism as a characteristic to be admired before the turn of the century. A very great strength of German and Japanese businesses has always been their emphasis on the group. While they retained an admiration for entrepreneurial traits in the individual, they have benefited from the synergy of the group and its cohesive force within the firm. There was in these successful economies co-operative effort not only within the firm but between firms.

In America, which like Britain had displayed very strong individualistic tendencies in the nineteenth century, individual goals became much more attuned to corporate goals. The large corporation, it has been argued, had accommodated the need for security and prestige, within the organisation.[13] Pressures in Britain to move out of this so-called 'primitive individualism' built up as competition mounted, but where the strongest pressure might have emerged – from government – it did not.

These strongly individualistic self-made men left an imprint on the culture of their society and of their firms. It has long been understood that not only a society but the sub-groups in society, including business organisations, develop a culture which can be distinguished from others. 'Culture' has been defined by Hofstede, in his work on the differences in national culture among forty modern nations, as 'collective programming of the mind', and values, which are among the building blocks of culture, as 'a broad tendency to prefer certain states of affairs over others'.[14] It is clear that a company builds up a framework of ideas, assumptions, and style of working, which can be called its culture or personality. There is often an acknowledgement by managements that the management style and certain policies, perhaps on training, are part of what constitutes their own firm, and that these have been much influenced by the attitudes and activities of past generations of managers, particularly the founders or other strong personalities. Hofstede's own study of a major American-based multinational found that its high level of concern for employee morale was historical: 'it grew out of the conviction of HERMES' founder many decades ago and was made one of the pillars of the HERMES way of life in which newcomers were automatically socialized'.[15]

In firms which have been successful, the earlier strategies which are thought to have contributed to that success can become part of an ideology, and thus very resistant to change even when they have ceased to be appropriate. In a recent study by Johnson of strategic decision-making in a men's retailing company, it was found that the original, successful strategy of the 1930s had been given the status of a failsafe device. It was turned to whenever the company was in difficulties, despite the very changed business conditions it experienced from the 1960s. The strategy of the company, Johnson argued, 'needs to be seen as substantially explained by its own history. The impact of the strategy of one period can be traced through to the strategy of another.'[16] The reverse may also happen. A firm may refuse to consider a strategy which failed it in the past, but which to new men seems now to have every chance of success.

The new men themselves are rarely in a position to resist absorbing the culture of the firm and its management style. The bulk of management training is carried out by existing managers on the job. The practices, policies, and beliefs of the management are passed on to the new men as the collective wisdom. New men entering the ranks of British management have normally spent all their business career in only one company, and only one function (see Chapter 6). They are likely, too, to have been chosen in the image of the old. They are chosen after all to 'fit in' with the existing management, not to undermine it. Suggestions for change are not always welcome. In the same recent study of a retail company, whose management was efficient by most criteria, it was recorded that 'when new management were introduced and voiced any dissent, such managers were re-educated into more acceptable ways of conceiving of problems most often by immersion in the day-to-day problems of doing things with their associated coping routines, or by being intimidated into accepting the ways of the organization'. Not only 'deviant' managers but consultants, too, were liable to find themselves subject to regulatory behaviour.[17]

The 'rational' element in business behaviour, which might have been expected to overcome the outdated beliefs and inappropriate modes of behaviour bequeathed to a firm, has been recognised as only one element, and not always the strongest element, informing business behaviour.

Exact criteria for 'rationality' are not often offered by those using the term. Rational and non-rational are sometimes used to convey meanings little different from logical and illogical. In economic theory a businessman is assumed to be acting rationally when he enlarges his output to the point at which his net profits are maximised. The model presupposes that the businessman has full information on which to act. It also presupposes that maximum profitability, rather than, for example, growth or security, is the normal aim of businessmen. 'Rationality' is used more generally by economic historians to indicate whether or not a businessman is making decisions which give priority to the firm's profitability in the context of existing business conditions, as the businessman understands them. Stress is always laid, very properly, on the constraints under which the businessman has to work.

The dangers inherent in this test are clear. Firstly, it is difficult to guard against imputing causality to effect. Nineteenth-century businessmen may have chosen, for example, after much investigation into the new technologies and the costs and benefits of making changes compared to not making changes, to stay with their existing machinery and methods. On the other hand, they may have made no such analysis and strategic decision, but through complacency, ignorance, inertia, expediency, or some other failing, merely continued with the old ways. The fact of their continuing to make profits is not sufficient evidence that this was the result of rationality. Secondly, rationality in this sense allows a short time-scale. This has been acknowledged, for example by Thomas:

The British economy did decline after 1900, relative both to historical and contemporary international experience. No doubt part of this was due to institutional rigidities and poor decisions by economic actors. Nevertheless, by and large, few mistakes were made. The economy continued to follow the dictates of comparative advantage, maximising current income if not long-term growth. Victorian entrepreneurs followed their instincts within the particular shape of factor constraints of the time and made choices that were, by and large, sensible given their criteria for success ... . However, from a longer perspective, rationality is not its own reward.[18]

But long-term strategies are equally a part of management's duties. British businessmen themselves have accepted that their firms, if at all possible, should continue into the future. They have demonstrated the strong importance they attach to the survival of companies, whether large or small. It has, for example, been a feature of the British economy that even failing companies with no prospects have been kept alive for extensive periods of time. And according to a recent set of guidelines for company directors,

It is implicitly assumed that companies, as organic creations possessed, through the device of incorporation, with potential immortality, have the overriding aims of survival and growth, and to achieve them they must both make profits and adapt to changing conditions. The implicit assumption about continuity is so strong that a company formed for a limited purpose ... will normally emphasise this unusual feature.[19]

To ensure future survival and growth, as the Institute of Directors noted, firms must adapt to changing conditions. They must also make profits, but a sufficient part of today's profits must be forgone or invested to help ensure that the firm does have a future.

A number of studies from as early as the 1950s have emphasised that rationality in any sense is only one element in business decision-making and that that element might be very weak.[20] The first substantial empirical study of managers at work, by Mintzberg in 1973, emphasised the importance of the values of those within the organisation, plus the manager's extensive knowledge of the organisation and its environment, for the success of any proposal.[21] Whilst managers do act rationally, there is also ample evidence, according to Johnson, 'that they also act politically, and that management cognition plays an important part in the interpretation of situations and guiding managerial action'.[22]

Any proposal to an employer to reform the practices which produced the organisation's managers faced, most importantly, restraint in terms of the long-term nature of the investment, which was of particular significance in British firms. British employers traditionally recruited men to a particular post to do a particular job. The onus was on the applicant (from inside or outside the firm) to convince the employer that he was already capable, through his education and previous experience (primarily his previous experience), of taking the job on. The employer was only prepared to allow a short period of on-the-job training. The emphasis was on the job, not the man, and on the present vacancy, not the potential of the candidate for the longer term. A firm might be willing to increase the level of education it demanded of new recruits, and to increase the number of days' training it allowed existing men. This did not greatly disturb existing practices, or the organisation. However, a management-power policy designed to raise the overall quality of management demanded not only that the employer accepted the short-term costs – the financial costs, the resistance of existing members of staff who might lose out in the reform, and the disruption which would be suffered until the new system was running smoothly – but it also required that management sustained a belief in the potential benefits of the new approach over a long time-scale, which might include a period of recession. But British employers preferred cutbacks rather than continuity when orders fell off.

British employers who have chosen, often for larger strategic reasons, to take management formation seriously have adopted some variation of a system which demanded above all a long-term investment. The investment took the form of time, money, and effort spent in identifying men with the potential to work effectively as individual managers and as members of the management team in the firm's particular environment, and then developing their potential over the longer term. The two most important tools which employers used to this end were education and planned experience. How education and experience were used – what form the education and experience took, whether the recruits or the firm accepted responsibility for providing all or part of the programme, how much of it took place inside the firm and how much externally – varied from firm to firm and over time, but all schemes shared a number of the following characteristics.

Firms looked to education, firstly, to help them identify and attract to the firm those among the young who would be amongst the most productive. The most productive young people were seen to be amongst those who had already proved during their formative years that they were achievers, in non-academic as well as academic activities. Firms also required that a fair share of the most capable young people leaving education became available to them. The potential of education for influencing values and motivations has always been acknowledged, if not always welcomed, and the more astute employers have exploited it with great success.

In practice, they have not expected education to be perfectly attuned to their particular needs, but they have worked to influence it to become so. The most effective ways to influence educational institutions proved to be the regular recruitment of students, vacation work for students, continuing financial support for educational projects, good personal relationships with individual educators, and a marked lack of business interference in what were seen as internal matters. Emphasising the national good rather than the company good also helped to gain a positive response from education. The many firms which preferred either to ignore or just to criticise the influence of the educators, on the grounds that they were hostile towards business, were adopting an approach which gave industry the worst of all worlds. If an education system does not value the business world, then it devalues it: education as an influence is not neutral. Employers, for their part, were not exercising much business acumen in encouraging, if only by default, hostile attitudes to continue. Businessmen have normally been in a strong position, at least in their local communities, to alter hostile attitudes by establishing stronger links with educational institutions. Employers could only fairly complain if they had made a good effort to change what they felt was damaging to their businesses.

Education was also needed to help with the difficult judgement which had to be made, on whether the candidate was the right type of recruit for the firm. Firms looked to particular institutions for particular types of recruit. In selecting the type of institution, management was also selecting the type of socialisation they preferred their new recruits to have had as the starting-point for further moulding by the firm.

The type of school or university they attended, their achievements there, and the recommendation of their educators were the first of a growing number of filters that young people were put through. Firms began to set up selection boards, and to put candidates through different kinds of psychological and aptitude tests. All the selection tests were intended to guard against the firm making costly mistakes, as well as to help it pick out suitable men. Employers looked for men of individual excellence who would none the less, with training, learn to work well with others and fit into the existing management culture.

Once the young person had been identified as amongst the most productive, and recruited to the firm, employers used the second tool, planned experience, to develop their capacities. Planned experience was not the limited range of experiences prolonged over many years common in so many firms, but an active effort to exploit the potential of the men through periods of learning inhouse and geared to the needs of the organisation. It included an early period under instruction in one or more of the various functions of the firm and general management, in home as well as foreign bases. If the men showed initiative, they were offered early responsibility, as an assistant to a manager, or perhaps as a junior executive with his own job, or as a leader of a small new project. Then they were allowed continuing opportunities to develop their capacities in the service of the firm. In some systems each recruit had a tailor-made individual programme prepared and supervised by a management development officer, and which included short internal and external courses to supplement on-the-job training. New men were required to have already, or be prepared to acquire, an understanding of business and business techniques. As they moved up the promotion ladder, they were expected to show improving analytical, interpersonal, and entrepreneurial abilities on the job. Promotion policies which were well constructed made it possible for each recruit to see a route upwards and equally possible for management to be able to use the exceptional man without difficulty. Recruitment from outside the firm was always an option, but the practice introduced many uncertainties and was used sparingly.

In Britain, as in Germany, the United States, and Japan, it was the largest organisations which invested in management systematically and which set the pattern for production of the nation's managers. It will be seen in the following chapters, however, that in these other countries there was a much wider acceptance than was apparent in the UK that the production of efficient managers was a management task. This acceptance extended down to larger numbers of medium-sized companies. It was more widely expected in competing economies that candidates should have benefited from what the education system could offer. Inside the firm, recruits were more likely to have received sufficient practical training for the work they had to do, and encouragement to develop their capabilities.

Chapter 2, which follows, shows that these three major competing nations shared a growing faith in the value of education from the nineteenth century when they began to produce their own corporate managers, and this faith remained a marked characteristic of the successful systems which they established over the following decades.

The practices widely adopted in the UK are analysed in Chapter 3. This shows that while foreign managers were being considered as a valuable resource and benefiting from significant investment in their abilities, British managers on the whole were not. Their formal education may or may not have had some bearing on a business career. They might or might not have acquired positive attitudes towards industry. Inside the firm they might or might not have undergone a programme of training for their present position or for higher responsibility.

The criticism of late nineteenth-century British businessmen, and their successors, is not that they did not match the best in competing countries, but rather that too few of them did so. And the majority are not accused of absolute, but of comparative, failure. There were only a small number of employers who were prepared to follow the lead of those who were investing in management, and this ensured that the criticism of Britain's managers remained at a high level.

References
(published in London unless otherwise stated)

1 M. Ackrill, 'Britain's managers and the British economy, 1870s to the 1980s', *Oxford Review of Economic Policy*, IV, 1, 1988, p. 72.

2 A. D. Chandler, Jr, *Scale and Scope: the Dynamics of Industrial Capitalism*, Harvard University Press, Cambridge, MA, 1990.

3 N. Crafts, 'The assessment: British economic growth over the long run', *Oxford Review of Economic Policy*, IV, 1, 1988, p. xiii.

4 S. Solomou and M. Weale, 'Balanced estimates of UK GDP 1870–1913', *Explorations in Economic History*, XXVIII, January 1991.

5 Crafts, 'The assessment', p. iv.

6 M. Thomas, 'Slowdown in the pre-World War One economy', *Oxford Review of Economic Policy*, IV, 1, 1988, p. 20.

7 Chandler, *Scale and Scope*, p. 268.

8 R. C. O. Matthews, C. H. Feinstein and J. C. Odling-Smee, *British Economic Growth 1856–1973*, Clarendon Press, Oxford, 1982, p. 451.

9 P. M. Hohenberg, *Chemicals in Western Europe 1850–1914*,

Rand McNally, Chicago, IL, 1967, p. 140.

10 G. Jones, ed., *British Multinationals: Origins, Management and Performance*, Gower, 1986, p. 20.

11 D. Marquand, *The Unprincipled Society: New Demands and Old Politics*, Jonathan Cape, 1988, p. 8.

12 D. C. Coleman and C. McCleod, 'Attitudes to new techniques: British businessmen, 1800–1950', *Economic History Review*, XXXIX, 1986, p. 600.

13 W. Lazonick, 'Strategy, structure, and management development in the United States and Britain', in K. Kobayashi and H. Morikawa, eds., *Development of Managerial Enterprise*, University of Tokyo Press, Tokyo, 1986.

14 G. Hofstede, *Culture's Consequences: International Differences in Work-Related Values*, Sage Pubns, 1980.

15 Hofstede, *Culture's Consequences*, p. 57.

16 G. Johnson, *Strategic Change and the Management Process*, Basil Blackwell, Oxford, 1987, p. 203.

17 Johnson, *Strategic Change*, pp. 229, 215.

18 Thomas, 'Slowdown', p. 22.

19 Institute of Directors, *Guidelines for Directors: Recommendations and Guidance on Boardroom Practice*, 1985, p. 7.

20 R. Stewart, *The Reality of Management*, Pan, 1967, p. 81.

21 H. Mintzberg, *The Nature of Managerial Work*, Harper and Row, New York, 1973, p. 89.

22 Johnson, *Strategic Change*, p. 188.

Chapter 2

Making able managers in Germany, the United States, and Japan

Germany

Bismarck's dictum that 'the nation that has the schools, has the future' was characteristic not only of the man but of the country he dominated. The Germans had needed no sudden and difficult conversion to see the value of education, general as well as vocational, for Germany's economic development. They had invested in education from the late eighteenth century, the years of Germany's first industrial stirrings, and over a century before the country had reached its position of world pre-eminence in many areas of high-technology manufacture. Saxony, for example, had started on the creation of trade schools in the eighteenth century, and, according to the British economist Alfred Marshall, had a superb system of education and a highly literate labouring and managerial force in 1812.[1] There were technical schools and polytechnics in several states by mid-century, and they prospered with the support of industrialists and the engineering profession. The State then combined with private initiative to achieve a vastly expanded system to assist with the vastly expanded needs of German industry. By 1905,

the Reich could offer a system of vocational education, matching a technical school against virtually every rung of the conventional education 'ladder'. Commercial and industrial 'continuation' schools were provided alongside the general primary schools, higher commercial and industrial schools alongside the general secondary schools, and the great technical high schools, the *technische hochschulen*, on a par with the universities.[2]

The universities had not been immediately responsive to the

17

needs of industrialisation. German universities had earned international fame for the quality of their scientific teaching and their stress on scientific research, while standing apart from work that was intentionally industry-related. Scientific research was considered an essential way to promote education, not the mere solving of practical problems. The universities expanded the amount and range of their work which industry could exploit – in textiles, glass, steel, dyestuffs, and agricultural chemicals[3] – but the professors remained deeply opposed to measures that appeared to threaten their prestige as guardians of scholarship. It was left to the technical schools to help train technical workers and managers for industry. The support for these institutions from engineers, industrialists, and the State was such that in 1899, over the objection of the university professors, the Emperor granted them the final accolade of the right to grant doctorates.

By the turn of the century, German industrialists, after some hesitation, were beginning to send their heirs to study in these technical universities.[4] Soon, engineers were replacing practical managers and foremen in workshops and factories. Engineers with doctoral degrees began to rise to the top of firms as members of their executive or supervisory boards. Engineers headed the largest electrical combines. They were joined at the top by trained chemists. From the 1850s industry had employed increasingly large research teams in well-equipped industrial research laboratories, particularly in the areas of metal production, chemicals, and electrical engineering. These teams aimed to perfect techniques for the profitable exploitation of marketable products and processes in German firms. Many of these products and processes had originally been discovered in the UK and elsewhere: the Germans had decided, as did the Japanese later, that the best way to move ahead was to implement quickly and improve upon with some vigour what was already known. By 1900 German chemical firms were deploying research groups of between fifty and seventy members, allowing them to carry out what research they wished, and expecting to discard 90 per cent of the results.[5] The heads of these research departments found themselves in a favourable track to the highest levels of management.

There was some contemporary criticism of the degree of regimentation and standardisation incorporated into the German education system, particularly for technical men, but the system seemed to accord well with the needs of industry. 'The narrow division of labour employed in German factories did in fact *require* highly specialized (or tightly focused) technicians. Similarly, a technology that was naturally imitative needed industrial researchers and managers who could produce adaptative innovations rather than make penetrating insights into new principles.'[6]

The high-grade commercial schools (*Handelshochschulen*), although they had been set up and financed largely by merchant guilds and chambers of commerce, received less state and business support in their early years. Businesses saw no particular need for graduates from high-level commercial schools when they had supplies of men with a good general education from the secondary grammar schools and men with a vocational training from the secondary commercial schools. German industry was composed primarily of very large businesses on the one hand and numerous small firms on the other. Large enterprises tended to be organised and administered like a state bureaucracy, with written procedures and a carefully defined hierarchy. Business functions were becoming more and more separated and specialised. The secondary-school men busied themselves with improving the systems in their specialisms, and at the top level, managers were expected to concentrate on entrepreneurial activities. The small firms for their part were, after the 1870s, very inclined to join one of the numerous cartels emerging to control prices and markets. In this way they became members of a body of national significance, and the cartels handled the members' financial, technical, and policy matters.

Business became slowly more supportive of the higher commercial schools after their decision to develop business, or enterprise, economics (called *Betriebswirtschaftslehre*), which drew on accounting and economic theory, for use as a form of management control.[7] The teaching of business economics later included the theoretical underpinnings of the major business functions of finance and marketing, then company organisation and control. It dealt separately with the various branches of business: industry, trade, insurance, banking, and so on. In the 1920s and 1930s, when industry experienced a strong need for cost accountants, auditors, and other commercial specialists, employers turned more strongly to these schools. The faculty became more confident, and they extended the time required to complete the course of a first degree from two years to three (and after the Second World War to four years and then five). Their success was such that in the inter-war period many of the higher commercial schools achieved university standing, and business economics began to join engineering and law as a popular choice for business candidates. Firms co-operated by providing the necessary work placements, by providing teachers, and financial support. 'Spurred by such competition, other Hochschulen were forced to concern themselves with business economics.'[8]

The education system in Germany had accepted the task of producing an educated and trained work-force for German industry through a comprehensive system of general and technical schools, and of developing the individual capabilities of prospective businessmen. But it did not, in contrast to the UK, expect to use the ancient world and its philosophies for the purpose, but the world of business and its enterprises. German firms, by the 1930s, attracted half the graduates of the *Hochschulen* and a smaller share of students from the universities themselves. German firms leaned heavily on education to provide them with the men they needed: they found it necessary to provide the new recruits with only limited amounts of practical experience to complete the training.

The educated German had very quickly begun to prove his worth. Well before the end of the nineteenth century German merchants were boosting trade through their knowledge of commercial affairs and foreign languages. German clerks were gaining valuable experience, and improving their languages, in French, Belgian, and English firms – the English took them on because they were cheap, and because language skills amongst Englishmen in business were very rare. German businesses had an abundance of men able to travel and start new branches abroad. And out of the strong scientific base laid down in the nineteenth century soon emerged Germany's impressive, and feared, electrical and chemical industries. Germany had moved with comparative ease into the new high-technology manufactures. The German electrical engineering industry, 'the biggest and costliest of the newcomers, began its expansion only in the 1880s, but by 1913 easily led the world schedule of exporters, controlling over half the international trade in electrical products'. The German chemical industry 'constructed a virtually complete monopoly of the European commerce in fine chemicals'. In dyestuffs, 'German pre-eminence was again global, and especially unchallengeable; by the early 1900s the Reich economy housed no less than eighty per cent of all world production in these commodities.'[9] Germany had achieved its first economic miracle before the First World War.

There were, of course, many factors contributing to Germany's success, apart from its educated managers and skilled work-force. There were the giant cartels and syndicates. According to Trebilcock, in nineteenth-century Germany these had prospered at some cost to the State, but with the new code of conduct in the early 1900s there emerged a system which encouraged a great advance in exports.[10] Similarly, the great German investment banks had invested in, and moved into the control and promotion of, German industrial enterprises. Cartels of banks were set up for the exploitation of particular industries. There was great competition between the Great Banks, but bank syndicates came into being for special long-term purposes. Moreover, the very large enterprise provided particular opportunities for the educated manager to use his capabilities. The German business environment produced few entrepreneurs of the outstanding, heroic type which was emerging in the USA, but the large organisation could still offer entrepreneurial opportunities, the necessary social status, and the chance to work in a strong management team to the willing German. The team element, already so pronounced within German research activity, had spread to dominate German management also.[11] There were sympathetic cultural attitudes prevailing, since

Germany possessed a set of past attitudes and role expectations centred on respect for the state and for military achievement which could be translated productively into industrial terms. Particular traditions could be utilized to connect large-scale industry with national objectives, thus providing an *alternative* to the equally traditional, but far more constraining, familial goals of the small producers.[12]

Education was, therefore, only one factor in Germany's rise to European pre-eminence before 1914; and the future was not Germany's as Bismarck had prophesied – its political leaders had thrown the chance away with two world wars – but the schools had served industry well. For its part industry had had the sense to exploit education, and to carry on where education left off in the making of able managers.

After the Second World War, German firms continued to acknowledge the value of higher education in producing their business leaders. In the mid-1950s men making their career in
business, or in any other high-level occupation in Germany, were
expected to have had a college-level, relevant education. They then
started their career at the bottom of the managerial hierarchy, with
the benefit of on-the-job training. The German concern not to
inhibit entrepreneurial flair and 'innate' qualities of leadership
coexisted happily enough with their admiration for trained competence. Promotion – step by step through the company's hierarchy – depended primarily on performance inside a specialism.
'Or if promotion takes into account personality values, the "personalities" at any rate seem preferentially selected from among
graduates in law, technical sciences, and economics. Candidates
from such non-professional fields as philosophy, music, education,
have significantly less chances – however great the "personality
value" of such graduates may be.'[13] A sample of 14,221 managers
in manufacturing industry in the 1960s found that 58 per cent held
a degree – 39 per cent of which were in engineering from either a
university or a *Hochschule*.[14]

Smaller firms were not excluded from all this activity. The
chambers of commerce, which were financed by compulsory subscriptions, were able to identify the best practices in the larger
companies and pass them on to the smaller through specially
constructed training programmes.

When in the mid-1950s German business found itself very short
of manpower for present and future management, rather than
decide that with so few managers it was much too busy to spare
the time to train more men, it instigated a large programme of
training. Germany's great industrial success in the nineteenth century and its post-1945 economic miracle were in the hands of a
business leadership which turned heavily *towards* education rather
than away from it when difficulties appeared.

However, there was some concern now that the long vocation-
ally-relevant education, and the rather narrow career channels,
encouraged in German managers too narrow a view of management issues for the modern world. And engineers 'needed a thorough complement of certain business administration knowledge, in
order to occupy some managerial functions, particularly in the
planning and construction of costly investment in capital-intensive

industries'.[15] The technical universities responded with hybrid courses. For business and economics graduates, the growing emphasis on economic theory and the theory behind the various business functions in German university courses was much criticised; and there were no courses for practising managers in German higher education. The American idea of formal education in business leadership, in marketing, and in the social sciences, was becoming more attractive. Efforts were made to introduce American-type, post-experience, business administration courses to broaden the outlook of the men on their way to the top. It was found that the Harvard-style degree courses did not suit the German situation. A long post-experience course outside the firm, after the long period of higher education, pleased neither the firm nor the young executives. Firms turned instead to increased amounts of internal training, and external training in extra-mural, non-academic management centres. The German system, however, continued to produce specialists, and has continued to be criticised on that account.

The United States

Except in the depressed years of the early 1930s, there has been no large question-mark hovering over the American manager. The most successful of them have been regarded, provided, that is, they stayed within the anti-trust laws, as heroes and a fount of all wisdom. From Henry Ford I to Lee Iacocca, they have been pressed to run for the presidency of the United States, although, as Carnegie noted in the 1890s, 'our rich men are not interested in public affairs: they leave that to men who can't succeed in business'.[16] US managers have been very much admired for their aggressive approach to getting the job done, and their eagerness to innovate. They have had the advantage of an environment which admired business success (and even accepted business failure), but they have also had great benefits from either education or experience or both.

Like practical ability in England, initiative and drive were the characteristics most admired by businessmen in nineteenth-century America. There was a widespread belief that education was the right of all the people, but formal educational qualifications played little part in employment prospects. The mid-century initiatives to provide schools for the practical application of science received scant support. American business heirs who wanted higher education went to the much-acclaimed German universities to study scientific method, and the American mechanic was left to learn his trade on the job, with the assistance of a mechanical institute. Experienced engineers were imported from England when engineers were required. But a leap forward for engineering came in 1862 with the US Administration's decision to grant federal aid for state colleges. Land-grant colleges multiplied, and began to develop engineering education. Another leap forward came when successful American businessmen, like Carnegie, began to take on, and demand more of, the men who had been through the engineering schools. Carnegie took large numbers of chemists and metallurgists from the Boston Institute of Technology and civil engineers from Troy, New York, immediately on graduation.

Business demand was such that, by the end of the nineteenth century, and despite its lower academic status, engineering was attracting a good share of the young of the middle and upper classes.[17] As in Germany, trained engineers were not barred from the top level of management, and they were heading some of the very largest corporations in the 1920s.[18] A study at the end of the 1920s noted that 404 establishments in the rubber, chemical, and electrical manufacturing industries employed a total of 35,447 men classified as 'executives', and of these, 11,764 were college and university graduates. Over 80 per cent were technical graduates. Advancement to executive ranks in manufacturing and other productive enterprises had been, it was found, largely through the operating and technical departments.[19] In the late 1920s, too, business demand for engineering graduates, particularly in chemicals, electricals, and motor vehicle manufacture, was such that demand outstripped supply. Demand for the science graduate was slower since there was still some uncertainty about his role in the firm.[20]

Industry had found that the school-trained man was not well equipped for industrial work. The equipment in most schools was less well advanced than in the large corporations and school engineering had veered more and more away from the practical towards the academic. US firms showed themselves willing to supplement the work done by the education system to get the skills they wanted. They began to set up their own schools to update the men's theoretical training and to teach practical application.[21] They also co-operated with, and tried to influence, the work of the schools and colleges. Engineering managers and engineering teachers found it advantageous to both sides to co-operate to advance engineering and engineering-based occupations. They worked together on joint research programmes and the joint study/experience courses for undergraduates. American industry, excepting the railways, which soon lost their appeal to the young, had had little difficulty in attracting college men into its ranks.

The existence of 'professional' associations in the US proved to be supportive to college education for business careers. American professional associations did not restrict and control the development of their specialism largely outside the higher education system. Rather they saw the existence of relevant courses in colleges and universities as crucial to the status of their association, and they made sure their subject was made available to students. The co-operation of practitioners and teachers made it easier for education to offer 'professional' business courses. The professional associations' governing bodies also tried to broaden their appeal, to draw in other groups. There was much less of the tendency of UK associations to exclusivity and factionalism. General managers, for example, formed the American Management Association in 1925, and it 'quickly became the leading professional organization for top and middle management in American business corporations. Its meetings and its publications focused on the overall administration, operation and control of the modern business enterprise.'[22]

There was little business enthusiasm initially for formal business education. University-level business education began in 1881 with the establishment of the Wharton School at the University of Pennsylvania, but US business was not yet interested. Three more universities made an offering before 1900, but raised no excitement. Then business did start to become interested. The US already had some very large companies before the 1880s, but many more appeared in the merger wave of the 1880s and 1890s over a number of industries, and managements began looking for better ways to direct and control them. They first felt a need for better-trained accountants and then for men not necessarily with specialist skills but with the potential to make a contribution to their fast-expanding enterprises. The higher education system responded eagerly to the growing demand, with perhaps thirty schools by the First World War. In 1915 there were around 10,000 students majoring in the commercial curricula of the colleges and universities: there were nearly 60,000 in 1926. By the mid-1920s 87 universities offered courses in commerce and business administration. First degrees in commerce rose from under 1,000 before the First World War to 6,621 in 1927–28.[23] The total student enrolment in commerce was now six times that of 1915 (the total student enrolment for all subjects was two and a half times that of 1915). In 1932, 400 colleges and universities (about half the total) had business courses. Organised university business courses were now enrolling over 90,000 students a year. The American schools of engineering had taken up the study of business methods by this time, which, although it had not gone very far in American eyes, has been offered as an explanation why, in the United States, engineers usually exhibited a keener appreciation of the economic side of their work than their typical British counterparts.[24]

Initially, education scarcely knew what it should offer to prepare students for business careers, apart from accounting. The Harvard Graduate School of Business, which had become successful by the mid-1920s, had begun very uncertainly in 1908, with offerings of principles of accounting, commercial contracts, and economic resources of the United States.[25] By the First World War, it was offering marketing, factory management, accounting and statistics, business policy, and finance. These were taught not only through lectures but increasingly, in the 1920s, through classroom discussion of actual business problems gleaned from teachers with knowledge of industry and, later, from interested businessmen. Harvard soon moved towards the concept which made its name and its fortune – corporate administration. This particular school, a purely graduate one demanding two years' full-time enrolment, had laid firm foundations by the mid-1920s, enough for interested educators in the UK to make the long trip over to see for themselves. In the early 1930s it was graduating around 400 MBAs a year. Other US schools had begun offering courses in the field of business organisation and management (which they described as being from the standpoint of general management), and then they added courses in marketing management, financial management, sales management, credit management, and others. Many schools already offered a general business course for the majority of undergraduates who had not yet made a vocational choice, as well as the more specialised courses for those who had made up their minds.

The great expansion of business education between the wars might obscure the fact that it had had to overcome very strong academic resistance in its early years. In the 1920s many liberal arts departments and engineering school faculties were still reluctant to co-operate with schools of business trying to construct the new interdisciplinary courses which were being offered to potential businessmen. For example, the measuring tools seen to be needed by firms required contributions from mathematics, accounting, and statistics: an understanding of the social setting of business required contributions from similarly diverse sources. Business education had been helped by the great expansion of US higher education from the 1900s, but much more so by the growing acceptance of business graduates by industry. In the 1920s, when the demand for technical graduates could not be satisfied, industry took on larger numbers of business graduates, not only in accounts, finance, selling, and personnel, but in the operating divisions. In a study in 1931 of Wharton School graduates, about 17 per cent reported that they were engaged in operating and production work in manufacturing firms. Business-school graduates and technical graduates were in competition for the higher executive positions.[26] The Bell System in the 1920s was recruiting 900 to 1,200 college graduates a year, a high proportion of them commerce graduates.[27]

Only a small proportion of managerial posts in American firms were occupied by university graduates until after the Second World War, but business education had come to be viewed by students and employers alike as a help towards a business career. An English, and very envious, educator wrote in 1932 that business education in the US had the support of much university opinion and a large section of the business community. Comparing this with the English scene, he wrote, 'No one can visit these large American schools of business without feeling some misgivings on the industrial future of any country which lacks them.'[28]

As with the engineers, US firms were willing to take promising raw material and give it opportunities to develop. Large industrial corporations had begun to use induction courses, with the object of creating integrated managers, before the First World War, and these became more widespread in the 1920s.[29] Also in the 1920s large US firms, in addition to supporting business schools, were extending their own training to cover junior executives and even senior men. Promotion in American firms came more with performance than either educational qualifications, social class, or nepotism, and in-house training was aimed at helping performance. General Motors' own Institute of Technology developed courses for both junior and senior executives. The programme for junior men took two years, six hours a week, and they were taught English, public speaking, practical economics, and psychology in Year One. Year Two covered accounting, efficiency, salesmanship, costs and control, and principles of instruction. Senior men attended classes for four hours a week. Year One included techniques of executive control, materials of engineering, and department management. In Year Two students covered business law, business cycles and statistics, factory organisation, and modern industrial tendencies. 'Scientific management' as a business philosophy had by now taken a back seat behind 'human relations', and the in-house programmes were expected primarily to develop the capacity to influence human behaviour, plus the ability to communicate both orally and by the written word.

American firms, not unusually, demanded loyalty. But this did not bar an aspiring manager from gaining experience in other firms. The ambitious man in the US was able to move from firm to firm to gain experience and promotion, if it was not available in only one. This planned experience by the individual was accepted as an asset and not as an indication that the man was inherently disloyal. New university men usually started in a function appropriate to their studies – although business graduates were not strongly averse to moving into operating and production work. The operating and technical departments were good springboards into senior management ranks, and business-school and technical graduates often competed for the same positions. They had similar occupational goals.

In spite of all the efforts exerted to produce able executives, and the admiration in which the American business schools were held abroad, US firms decided, as had German firms, that the strong pull towards the specialisms was hindering the development of wider managerial capabilities. The corporations tried even harder after the Second World War to counter this by increasing their use of formal education. Business education of all kinds experienced a veritable explosion of courses in the post-war period.

American firms had channelled money into the education system since the beginning of the century, and made their organisations available to students. In this way they ensured that a sufficient part of the system offered an education that was broadly based as well as vocationally orientated and sympathetic to the business world. In-house training had also been costly of time and money. Yet US firms knew no more than did British firms how to quantify the returns on this huge outlay of resources. But what they did accept was that exceptional men were more likely to appear if exceptional efforts were made to produce them.

Japan

In a Confucian society, as is well known, a person's worth is related much more to the amount of education he has received than to the level of his social class or bank balance. Confucian tradition in Japan had encouraged a respect for learning which was deeply rooted, and already infused with a curiosity towards the new and the unusual, before the 1860s and the decision to industrialise.[30] This consensus towards education was a potential weapon in the cause of modernisation which the Japanese government and business leaders were not slow to exploit.

The decision to modernise Japan, along the lines of the technically superior (albeit 'dirty and ill-mannered') European countries, was taken soon after the restoration of Emperor Meiji in 1868. From that time the Japanese began studying, copying, and adapting what was best in the West for Japan's purposes, although initially they had to rely heavily on foreign experts as both practitioners and teachers. The continual bullying by the Americans and Europeans had helped to convince the oligarchy that Japan had to aim for 'a rich country and a strong army'. It was a brave decision, given the isolation and poverty of much of the country, and a very hard one for the peasantry – upon whose backs much of the financial burden would fall.

The early moves into industrialisation in Japan were state-led and directed, but the response of the private sector was crucial thereafter. The government took upon itself the task of setting up enterprises in strategically important industries – mining, shipbuilding, railways, steel manufacture – but its foremost strategy soon settled down to one of assisting private concerns to move ahead. Japanese entrepreneurs moved happily and successfully into light industry, particularly cotton textiles, which became an early success story for Japan. With generous government support a small number of enterprising, family-owned concerns came to dominate the economy. Much of Japan's initial and impressive growth has been attributed to these very large, very diversified, and centrally-controlled 'zaibatsu' (holding companies). The zaibatsu, with their immediate and growing need for expertise, soon turned to education to help them acquire skilled employees. From the early years of industrialisation, Japan saw education as largely the servant of industry and the State, and education was moulded accordingly. The new Meiji government wanted a literate populace and a steady supply of the business and political leaders that the country would need.

The modernisation of Japanese education was already under way before the Restoration. Curiosity about Western technology had been growing alongside the continuing interest in such traditional educational subjects as Chinese literature, calligraphy, and Confucian ethics. But the new ideas, which emphasised the practicality of education rather than its contribution to character-building, were generally greeted with loathing. Western scientific teaching seemed appropriate only for barbarians. But, as in Germany, the US, and to some extent Britain, the modernisers were winning through by the end of the century. In Japan, the retention of moral training based on Confucian ethics helped the Japanese to accept the changeover. Similarly, traditional values – respect for family and group, service to Emperor and country, physical fitness – became modern values. And non-vocational studies survived: the new Imperial University, which made wide provision for Western literature, art, and pure science, sat at the top of the new educational pyramid.

The pyramid came to consist of a very firm base of compulsory elementary education for all. The brightest pupils were apportioned to a variety of secondary schools with the purposes of technical and vocational training; and depending on which track they had been placed in, students could find themselves in higher education to continue their training. A liberal education alone and without some vocational leanings was not considered sufficiently helpful, either to the student, to industry, or to the State. In the early years institutions were set up when they were required, for example, to train agricultural experts, engineers, or bank clerks. Japan established a business school in 1875, using private funds. In 1877 it founded its first modern engineering college, using the energies of a Scot (Henry Dyer) and the best ideas of the German education system. By the 1880s, Japan had the largest English-speaking technical university in the world. In the early years of the twentieth century Japan (combining state and private effort) expanded the number of its higher commercial colleges, higher technical colleges, and imperial universities.

Western visitors soon noticed that Japan, although educationally still a long way behind Germany, France, and Switzerland, was well ahead of many Western countries in the quality and quantity of the provision it made. The private sector, always very important in education in pre-Meiji Japan, had moved in to help meet the growing demands of private industry, and private provision remained crucial. The cost of higher education to the State was not in fact very large: industry and students' families bore a major part of the burden of education.

Japanese entrepreneurs had not immediately seen a place for college graduates in their businesses. But attitudes had begun to change by the end of the nineteenth century. Japan's strategy for industrialisation – the wholesale copying and improving of Western techniques and technologies – demanded sufficient if not large numbers of technical experts, supported by much larger numbers of technicians of various kinds. The fast-growing zaibatsu, which imported Western machinery for Japanese firms, were the first to start recruiting college men. They needed men able to understand Western technology and advise their customers, and then they wanted more young men in leadership positions in the various zaibatsu companies who already understood modern business methods and technologies, or could be trained to understand them. Appropriate non-college men were just not available. The zaibatsu banks turned to the higher commercial schools for men who understood book-keeping, foreign exchange, foreign correspondence, and insurance. The principal course of study in the famous Higher Commercial College of Tokyo lasted for three years and it included many of the subjects offered on the Bachelor of Commerce degree courses in the UK at about the same time. These were commercial and industrial geography, commercial and industrial history, political economy, public finance, statistics, civil law, commercial law, international law, science of commerce, and languages. The Mitsui Trading Company, the first zaibatsu to start taking on college graduates, in the 1880s, had an amazing 731 of them by 1914.[31]

College graduates, for their part, initially preferred government service, but the emphasis on educational requirements for a business career, the ethical training, and the propaganda which insisted that industrial warriors were needed as much as military warriors helped make business more acceptable. Sons of the old warrior class, the samurai, who were already among the educated elite, found that banking at least was a sufficiently honourable occupation.

The graduates were a costly item for Japanese firms as salaries had to compete with those in government service, and the new men were used accordingly. They were first of all used to replace the well-paid foreign experts: they were cheaper and it was a very good move for national pride. Where industrial firms could not afford an engineer full-time, he was shared between a number, acting as a consultant rather than an employee. The zaibatsu groomed new men carefully. Well-educated recruits started in the zaibatsu bank, where they could get an overview of the whole enterprise and the position of each company within it. Then they moved into junior management in a branch of the bank to gain experience (a zaibatsu bank had a very close relationship with each of its companies). The men, having had a higher education relevant to business and experience in a management position, were then moved into the management of a zaibatsu firm. Their educational qualifications helped to legitimise their speedy promotion, but they had proved their worth. In the Mitsubishi group promising candidates were moved frequently, and across functions. They were expected to assume increasing responsibility and leadership, and 'to be ready to acquire new skills and knowledge'.[32] This proved an effective way of getting educated men more broadly into management positions in Japanese industry. Even later when seniority rules became widespread, educational qualifications remained important and often all the candidates for management were graduates. Large non-zaibatsu firms followed the example of the zaibatsu and began to employ commercial high-school students and then college graduates as potential managers. Some started as clerks and worked their way up, but those from prestigious colleges were immediately given responsibilities and a smooth route to the top.[33] Cotton spinning, so important to Japan's early growth, took graduates from the engineering faculties. By the First World War executive positions in the largest firms were falling to college men; and in the 1920s and 1930s it was more usual than not for Japanese businessmen to have a college degree: 'it was unusual to meet an officer of the banks, industrial companies or merchant houses who had not been trained, in a college or university, in subjects appropriate to his duties'.[34] It has been estimated that some 14 per cent of company presidents in large firms in Japan were graduates by 1913; that figure had reached around 70 per cent by 1930 (and 88 per cent by 1961).[35]

Once the path from the college or university to the zaibatsu had been opened up, it stayed open. Zaibatsu tended to prefer graduates from the one university of their choice, and a strong tie between the two institutions grew up. For their part, the students were well disposed towards the prestigious zaibatsu, where they would be welcomed into the group. The impressive growth of individual firms and industries in the early years of this century reflected well on the trained managers, and graduates became more certain of their status in a business career. The route into management in the largest firms had not taken long to be clearly laid out, well understood, and on the whole accepted.

Japan's economic growth from 1868 to the Second World War was substantial, but it had seen a financial crisis in 1914, stimulated by large military spending, and a sharp downturn in the 1920s. Despite the major economic boost of the First World War (Japan had supplied the Allied Powers), the economy entered a long depression in the 1920s. Japan, however, did not suddenly and sharply curtail its investment in education, as happened in Britain in the early 1920s. Japan's education system continued to expand at a rapid rate. Vocational training spread amongst the large firms and became more systematised: in-house training for all levels had become an essential element of manpower planning – and this despite the over-abundance of educated labour by this time.[36]

The over-supply was soon put to work. The depreciation of the yen encouraged growth, and Japan's wars in Manchuria, then with

China, demanded supplies. Heavy industry expanded and the country took a firm leap forward into the scientific age. The rapid expansion put a heavy strain on the managerial skills available. The old complex zaibatsu conglomerates were still held together by the original system of strong control, based on the tradition of family loyalty, at the centre, and delegation of authority to well-prepared and able managers in the individual firms. The so-called 'new' zaibatsu came into existence to cope with the large capital-intensive projects demanded by the military, and these needed many more experts and men who could co-ordinate from the centre. But the new zaibatsu found themselves unable to produce sufficient numbers of good managers in the time allowed. They used the raw material of intelligent men leaving the university with good grades in subjects relevant to industry – engineering, econ-omics, business studies – and this raw material they trained in-house. But they speeded up the process. As the growth of the new zaibatsu had been fast, 'there was no time to pay much attention to organisation, management or systematic central controls', and after the war, when the Allies demanded the break-up of all the zaibatsu, the companies of the older type were in a much better position to survive, though in different forms, than those of the newer, less stable group.[37]

After the Second World War, the Americans insisted that the Japanese education system, such a strong weapon in the hands of the government, be 'reformed', that is, be more democratic and less able to be manipulated for militaristic ends. The dual-track system (popular and elite) in schools was replaced by a single-track system and the universities were opened up to many more students. Ethics teaching was forbidden. The education system pre-1945 had been moulded to serve the requirements of the State and industry and it had proved very effective. Post-1945 the system changed, but by general consent the requirements of State and industry remained the main purpose of education in Japan. After the Second World War, Japan had realised that it was still techni-cally inferior to Western countries, and it began, as it had done in the 1860s, to learn from the West, and to adjust its education system. Japan determined to catch up with the West, and its educated people was its main asset. The pyramid was made larger and flatter. Educational facilities, both state and private, began to expand at a great rate. In 1950 there were 201 universities, compared with under fifty pre-war,[38] the largest number of students going into engineering, economics, and business administration. By 1955 there were 245 universities (and 379 by 1972). Competition for places, particularly in the institutions supplying the most prestigious firms, remained intense.

Over the decades formal schooling had become less and less concerned with vocational training. Companies increasingly wanted the system to produce highly educated and relevantly educated young people, preferring to do the vocational training themselves. The trend applied equally to the higher grades of recruits. It had developed before 1960 to the extent that university graduates were recruited not for specific responsibilities but only for either the technical side or the administrative side of business. An 'accountant' may never have taken a formal course in accounting.[39] Postgraduate courses were less important in the universities because of the investment industry was prepared to make in in-house training. Japanese enterprises fashioned their own specialists, and conducted their own research.

The high level of investment in educated personnel, together with lifelong employment for them from the 1920s, had the effect of binding employer and employee. There were costs to both sides. The employer was disinclined to sack even in a downturn and the employee, with what became increasingly non-transferable skills, was hardly equipped to change employer. But long-term employment did allow a high level of planning and training for management succession, and it did take out the terrible uncertainty widely associated with employment in industry.

The Japanese education system was much criticised for the 'examination hell' it demanded and for the universities' control over entry into the largest firms. But it – the public and private sectors combined – supplied Japanese firms with what they had the sense to demand. It trawled very effectively for talent amongst the populace. Japanese businessmen used the system to their good advantage, and they provided in-house what they felt the system was not capable of providing or what was done better in-house. Japan's prodigious economic success had less to do with miracles than its long-term and high-level commitment to trained intelligence.

References

1 C. Trebilcock, *The Industrialization of the Continental Powers 1780–1914*, Longman, 1981, p. 30.

2 Trebilcock, *The Industrialization*, p. 62.

3 Trebilcock, *The Industrialization*, p. 63.

4 J. Kocka, 'The rise of the modern industrial enterprise in Germany', in A. D. Chandler, Jr and H. Daems, eds., *Managerial Hierarchies: Comparative Perspectives on the Rise of the Modern Industrial Enterprise*, Harvard University Press, Cambridge, MA, 1980, p. 95.

5 Trebilcock, *The Industrialization*, p. 64.

6 Trebilcock, *The Industrialization*, p. 64.

7 R. K. Locke, *The End of the Practical Man: Entrepreneurship and Higher Education in Germany, France and Great Britain 1880–1940*, JAI Press, Greenwich, CT, 1984, p. 159.

8 H. Hartmann, *Education for Business Leadership: the Role of the German 'Hochschulen'*, OEEC, Paris, 1955, p. 24.

9 Trebilcock, *The Industrialization*, p. 47.

10 Trebilcock, *The Industrialization*, p. 73.

11 Trebilcock, *The Industrialization*, p. 65.

12 Trebilcock, *The Industrialization*, p. 66.

13 Hartmann, *Education for Business Leadership*, p. 20.

14 A. Sorge, 'The management tradition: a continental view', in M. Fores and I. Glover, eds., *Manufacturing and Management*, HMSO, p. 93.

15 Sorge, 'The management tradition', p. 97.

16 Diary of Beatrice Webb, 24 May 1898, available in LSE library.

17 D. F. Noble, *America by Design: Science, Technology, and the Rise of Corporate Capitalism*, Alfred A. Knopf, New York, 1977, p. 39.

18 A. D. Chandler, Jnr, *Strategy and Structure: Chapters in the History of the Industrial Enterprise*, MIT Press, Cambridge, MA, 1962, p. 317.

19 J. Bossard and J. F. Dewhurst, *University Education for Business*, University of Pennsylvania Press, Pennsylvania, PA, 1931, p. 39.

20 L. F. Haber, *The Chemical Industry 1900–1930*, Clarendon Press, Oxford, 1971, p. 364.

21 Noble, *America by Design*, p. 171.

22 A. D. Chandler, Jnr, *The Visible Hand: The Managerial Revolution in American Business*, Harvard University Press, Cambridge, MA, 1977, p. 466.

23 Bossard and Dewhurst, *University Education*, p. 255.

24 G. C. Allen, *The British Disease*, Institute of Economic Affairs, 1979 ed., p. 46.

25 M. T. Copeland, *And Mark an Era: The Story of the Harvard Business School*, Little, Brown and Co., Cambridge, MA, 1958, p. 22.

26 Bossard and Dewhurst, *University Education*, p. 40.

27 Bossard and Dewhurst, *University Education*, p. 44.

28 J. A. Bowie, *American Schools of Business*, Pitman, 1932, p. 10.

29 W. Lazonick, 'Strategy, structure, and management development in the United States and Britain', in K. Kobayashi and H. Morikawa, eds., *Development of Managerial Enterprise*, University of Tokyo Press, Tokyo, 1986, ch. 4.

30 G. C. Allen, 'Education, science and the economic development of Japan', *Oxford Review of Education*, IV, 1, 1978, p. 28.

31 S. Yonekawa, 'University graduates in Japanese enterprises before the Second World War', *Business History*, XXVI, July 1984, pp. 193–218.

32 E. Daito, 'Recruitment and training of middle managers in Japan, 1900–1930', in K. Kobayashi and H. Morikawa, eds., *Development of Managerial Enterprise*, University of Tokyo Press, Tokyo, 1986, p. 168.

33 J. Hirschmeier and T. Yui, *The Development of Japanese Business 1600–1973*, George Allen and Unwin, 1981 ed., p. 116.

34 Allen, *The British Disease*, p. 47.

35 C. Handy, *The Making of Managers*, NEDO, 1987, p. 86.

36 S. B. Levine and H. Kawada, *Human Resources in Japanese Industrial Development*, Princeton University Press, Princeton, NJ, 1980, p. 54.

37 Hirschmeier and Yui, *Development*, p. 175.

38 W. K. Cummings and I. Amano, 'Japanese higher education', in P. G. Altbach, ed., *Comparative Higher Education Abroad*, Praeger, New York, 1976, p. 228.

39 K. Azumi, *Higher Education and Business Recruitment in Japan*, Teachers College Press, New York, 1969, p. 55.

Chapter 3

Producing managers the British way

Britain's industrialisation had begun as early as the 1780s, and by the middle of the nineteenth century, when Germany and the US were just getting under way, it held a commanding lead over all others. It had reached this enviable position without the benefit of an education system, and with less scientific and technical training than that enjoyed by its less successful competitors, France and Germany. The technical inventions of the First Industrial Revolution had been 'exceedingly modest, and in no way beyond the scope of intelligent artisans experimenting in their workshops, or of the constructive capacities of carpenters, millwrights, and locksmiths ... . Even its scientifically most sophisticated machine, James Watt's rotary steam engine (1784), required no more physics than had been available for the best part of a century.'[1] Entry had been made even easier by the small initial capital outlay required.

At the height of its economic power Britain's industrial might had rested on a small number of giant industries – textiles, coal, and mechanical engineering. The British cotton industry, the first industry to be revolutionised, began as a by-product of colonial trade, and expanded dramatically as British industry established a monopoly in vast areas of semi-colonial and colonial markets. Raw cotton from the USA had become plentiful from the 1790s, and the new inventions which revolutionised manufacture were reasonably simple and cheap, and paid for themselves almost immediately in terms of higher output. 'They could be installed, if need be piecemeal, by small men who started off with a few borrowed pounds ... . The expansion of the industry could be financed easily out of current profits, for the combination of its vast market conquests and a steady price inflation produced fantastic rates of profit.'[2] Metals and machinery manufacture were stimulated by the existence of large quantities of coal and the reservoir of suitable craft skills which had built up in the long decades of semi-industrialisation before the 1780s.

Those had who made the business decisions which had contributed to Britain's enviable record had used their wits and what business acumen they could muster to exploit the advantages around them. Many had emerged from earlier merchanting, trading, and craft groupings. Some business families had actively prepared their successors by insisting on a period of apprenticeship in either the family firm or another. Sons of the enterprising Quaker community could attend the Nonconformist dissenting academies, which had a very practical emphasis and taught foreign languages, mathematics, accounting, and some science, or the Scottish universities.[3] Calvinist Scotland had 'sent a stream of brilliant, hard-working, career-seeking, and rationalist young men into the south country: James Watt, Thomas Telford, Loudon McAdam, James Mill'.[4] Later, keen young Englishmen interested in a scientific training journeyed to Germany. But overall, few of those in charge in British firms had had the help of, or perhaps much need for, formal education. An example, of the many that are available in obituary columns, will illustrate what was quite possible:

Mr. Thomas Charlesworth, of Leicester, was born in that town on December 5th, 1825. His parents were in humble circumstances; he received but a very slight education at the Great Meeting School, and at the age of nine began to work for his living at Mr. Bowmar's hosiery trimming factory, where he remained about 20 years.

In the year 1856 he commenced in a small way on his own account as a dyer and trimmer of hosiery goods, and by his industry, frugality, and aptitude, he succeeded far beyond his expectations.

His business continued to prosper until his death, which occurred on the 28th of May, 1876.[5]

Yet the lack of education already impressed foreigners. In 1839 a German commentator wrote:

it cannot but amaze us that a country in which the manufacturing tendencies are predominant, and hence the need to familiarize the people with the sciences and arts which advance these pursuits is evident, the absence of these subjects in the curriculum of youthful education is hardly noticed. It is equally astonishing how much is nevertheless achieved by men lacking any formal education for their professions.[6]

The continuing low level of education enjoyed by British businessmen was reflected in the continuing backwardness of the English education system. This applied to all levels of education, from primary through to undergraduate. As late as 1870, only 40 per cent of ten-year-olds and 2 per cent of fourteen-year-olds were officially receiving full-time education. In that year the State began to act as a direct provider of primary education to supplement the work of the voluntary sector, but not till 1880 was schooling made compulsory (for children up to ten years of age, and up to twelve years from 1899). Middle-class education (later called secondary education) had been of generally poor quality until the 1860s. The public and grammar schools had then begun to be reformed, but they still offered a narrow education. They concentrated on the study of Latin and Greek, to develop the intellect, and the participation in games and communal living, to develop both body and personality. Middle-class education, on grounds of cost as well as lack of inclination, had little use for such subjects as chemistry, mathematics, or modern languages. Facilities in England for technical education were very sparse until the 1880s when technical instruction at all levels received a major boost. Mounting pressure for improvements in technical educational facilities had at last succeeded in tapping various sources of funds. Most importantly, the wealthy City companies had become so anxious that their funds might be confiscated and reapplied, as was being threatened, to their original purpose of technical instruction, that they opened their vast coffers. They supported a wide range of initiatives, from evening classes for apprentices through to university education for technologists.

The university system, at the top of what was a confusing patchwork of educational facilities, still consisted of only two teaching universities and a small number of new, but struggling colleges offering university extension work and London degrees. In 1885 Germany, with a population of 45 million, had 24,187 university students. England, with a population of 26 million, had only 5,500.[7]

On the eve of the Second Industrial Revolution, British employers had demonstrated little interest in formal education, either general or technical, as an asset to young men in business. Learning through practical experience alone was still held to be the one best way for young men to learn and to prepare themselves for higher posts. And it was the young man's own responsibility to gain the necessary experience. Employers had not accepted that training was a task which ought to have much of their attention. Traditional apprenticeships for both the technical and commercial sides of the firm were still undertaken in many firms, but even here training was not considered to be a matter for managerial involvement: management was content to leave the preparation of the next generation of skilled men to the present generation of skilled workers. Thus, British industry still relied heavily for its continued vibrance on the initiative of individual young men to seek out the education they needed for their career, and the experience they needed to raise their own standard of performance. Ambitious young men moved from firm to firm in this country and overseas gaining experience, often experimenting with new systems and technologies along the way.

But the conditions which had allowed such a heavy dependence on the self-taught and self-trained, and which had also allowed the untaught and untrained to prosper, had begun to change long before the end of the nineteenth century. Businessmen were being told very bluntly well before the end of the nineteenth century that industry would need much better-educated men to lead it in the future, and that it would have to upgrade its business as well as its technical skills over a wide area if British firms were going to stay ahead of foreign competition. Competing nations, especially Germany, were investing impressively in skilled manpower, and reaping short-term as well as long-term benefits. Alongside their advances in science and technology, they were proving to be formidable at marketing their manufactured goods. British businessmen were urged to follow their lead in learning foreign languages and informing themselves to a much better degree on the changing needs of foreign customers. The occasional firm showed that it could match the best anywhere. 'Where some British industrialists lost trade because they would not redesign the wrapping of needles despatched to Brazil, others of their number could still redesign the world's biggest warship for the same market – and do it in Rio de Janeiro.' The firm attracting praise was Vickers.[8]

But there were too many firms like the needle manufacturers and they were too widespread for industry to have felt unjustly criticised. British firms were able to buy in language and commercial skills, as well as technical skills, but they were buying in on a scale that was causing concern. From the 1860s, English industry was dependent on German and Swiss talents in all levels of the enterprise.[9] The Chambers of Commerce warned in 1887 that

Our counting houses are filled with foreigners – for the most part Germans and German Jews – who are indebted for their position and advancement in life to the superior training and instruction which they have received. In all our large commercial centres, the sale of our products and manufactures is conducted largely by foreigners, and that much of the purchase of foreign goods is carried on through foreign houses and agents is well known to every commercial man. International financing and foreign banking business is almost entirely in their hands and it is also a well-known fact that these houses employ foreign clerks largely if not exclusively.[10]

It was argued that Englishmen were equally entitled to the superior training and instruction enjoyed by foreigners, and that the leading organisations could not leave it to chance to produce the trained managers which would be needed in the highest ranks of the larger and more complex firms of the future.

Some entrepreneurs were already making a marked investment in new men. They had grasped the opportunities which the new technologies and the resulting economies of scale allowed, and were investing in managerial teams accordingly. The most successful were in the food, drink, and tobacco industries which, with their relatively simple processes, did not require too great an investment in managerial hierarchies. But some, according to Chandler, were in industries with more complex technologies: 'British entrepreneurs did build the managerial teams necessary to compete effectively in a number of new, high-volume, capital-intensive industries, including rubber, glass, explosives, synthetic alkalies, and man-made fibers.'[11] The managerial teams were smaller than those found in the US and the owning families were able to remain in control, but these became successful firms in world markets. However, those firms which raised their investment in management to any marked degree were exceptional. And they were too few in number to influence the direction in which the majority of British employers were choosing to go.

British firms were choosing, firstly, to adopt strategies in these difficult times which would not require a significant investment in management. They preferred instead strategies which allowed them to continue with very small teams, under their own direction. In the 1890s, they responded to the more competitive business conditions, and to the commercial and financial opportunities which they had seen, with a high level of merger activity. In too many instances, however, few of the individual owning families seemed to have had the will or the intention of allowing a full merger, with the construction of a single, strong managerial organisation. What often emerged was a loosely-structured holding company which allowed every individual operating company to carry on, with the same small management team, in much the same way as before. This type of merger remained commonplace until the 1960s.

Similarly, British entrepreneurs resisted the lure of the funds available in the capital market to pursue growth, at the likely cost of losing personal control of the firm. What UK businessmen had discovered and much preferred was the private limited company. This allowed the existing owners the benefits of limited liability without the possible challenge to their control from outsider shareholders. The preference of family firms in the UK was to remain a family-owned and controlled enterprise, or at least to stay family dominated, with family and friends in the top jobs. If they sold their interests, it was not unusual for some of the family members to remain at their posts and family domination to continue much as before. A single member of the old family, if a respected member, could expect all other Board members to defer to his views.

The large British firms which did emerge did not reorganise for growth to the extent that was available to them, under larger teams of enterprising managers. Organisational change lay far behind what was being implemented abroad. The largest British firms slowly took up the functionally departmentalised form of organisation. The movement seems not to have gone so far even by the 1930s that all senior managers understood what was meant by it. At a meeting of representatives of large businesses in 1931, a Mr Meikle of Pilkington Bros. asked, 'Can you enlighten me on alternative systems of organisation, particularly "Functional Management". How would you apply it and what are its advantages?'

The meeting concluded that 'The greatest value of the discussion lay in the fact that it revealed an earnest desire on the part of most of those concerned to grapple with what was thought to be a new type of organisation, and to understand its application and uses.'[12] In the merger wave of the 1920s, a few firms – primarily ICI and Unilever – had begun moving towards the American type of divisionalised company structure which was serving companies like General Motors and du Pont so well; but not till the 1950s was there a real determination to take advantage of the potentialities of organisational change. British firms, as they expanded, chose either to strengthen their control from the centre but without expanding the managerial resources to do so, or simply to allow their grip over the various departments, branches, and subsidiaries to become looser. The small investment in managerial teams allowed, and required, the owners and their families (or, as sometimes happened, a non-owning dynasty) to continue to manage the firm in the personal way which they so much preferred. It has been judged that, 'What differentiated British entrepreneurial, later family-controlled, enterprises from those in the United States and Germany was that the entrepreneurs assembled smaller management teams, and until well after World War Two they and their heirs continued to play a larger role in the making of middle- and top-management decisions.'[13]

Alongside the continued preference for personal management (in the sense both of personal control and personal style of management[14]) with the concomitant smaller management teams, went a continued preference for the traditional practices which produced the succeeding generation of managers for British industry. There were, of course, only small numbers of managerial posts in British firms, at least until the 1930s when the numbers began to rise significantly. According to census data, there were in Britain 813,000 managers, administrators and higher professionals in 1911 (constituting 4.4 per cent of the occupied population), 1,010,000 in 1931 (4.8 per cent), 1,680,000 in 1951 (7.5 per cent), and 3,438,000 in 1981 (13.5 per cent). There were many reasons for the small numbers, apart from the continuing traditional structures of British firms which used small management teams. Until attitudes began to change in the 1930s, firms had a serious aversion to increasing the numbers of administrators: these were seen as constituting a heavy cost to the firm, not a means of aiding control and efficiency. The directors and senior managers normally involved themselves in the day-to-day running of the firm, preferring not to delegate and so create more positions with authority. The specialisation of management's tasks had not gone as far as it might in many instances: in much of British industry purchasing was still typically centred in the office of the production manager and selling was seen as a simple distributive function.[15] Some functions undertaken in foreign firms were not regarded as necessary in British ones, or were carried out by outside agencies. Industrial relations, which in large foreign firms might command an industrial relations department and perhaps an industrial relations director, was in Britain usually undertaken by an employers' association. The major change here did not come until the 1970s. Personnel managers were a rare breed before the Second World War. The men who rose to manage UK enterprises into the twentieth century emerged in ways which demonstrated strong continuity with the practices of the 1890s.

A prime source of men for management at the start of the period was patronage of one kind or another, and this was not really in full retreat until the 1950s. Its use was widespread in all types of firm and at all levels. The continuing strength of family-owned and family-dominated firms in Britain helped to ensure that it remained important throughout the inter-war period. Family firms had predominated in most branches of manufacturing before the First World War and remained important in a number of industries (like hosiery, steel, textiles, branded packaged products, publishing and retailing) until after the Second World War. Many of Britain's largest concerns in manufacturing, metal production and shipbuilding had remained under family management. In 1930, twenty-three out of the fifty largest UK manufacturing companies were owner-dominated; and in 1950, fifty of a sample of ninety-two large manufacturers were controlled by families, the number falling thereafter 'progressively but not substantially'.[16]

A family firm, it has to be said, gave the family social status and history in the community's eyes. To many family members, the firm was a way of life. It was also expected to be the source of an income large enough to keep them in the manner to which they had become accustomed. Thus the idea of preparing someone else's sons to take over the firm was entirely disliked. The ruling family network of J. Lyons, for example, had not considered allowing non-family managers into the highest level of control – which was not in this firm the Board but a body known as general management – as late as the 1950s. Whilst any member of the family in the company could expect by right to become a member of general management, no non-family member had ever been recruited. The tradition died only slowly thereafter.[17] The stockbroking firm of Foster and Braithwaite preferred until 1968 to lose good staff than to take non-family men into full partnership.[18] The building firm of Wates 'deliberately restricted the expansion of its business in the 1950s until the latest generation of the family was ready to move into commanding positions in the company and initiate a new phase of growth'.[19] Family influence remained into the 1960s a predominant factor in promotion in many small and medium-sized companies, although in large companies top posts were by now more genuinely open to outsiders.[20]

But patronage was not confined to family-owned or family-dominated companies. In 1918 both the London County Council and the new Federation of British Industries came to the conclusion that 'at present entrance to many occupations is haphazard and to a large extent the result of nomination and personal influence', and that 'a more scientific system should be set up, in which the attainments and abilities of the young persons individually may receive due consideration in their appointment to positions in Industry'.[21] The directors of large public companies in the 1920s and beyond expected to be able to resign in favour of sons or nephews.[22] In 1930 the Cadet Scheme of the Underground Railway, which had aimed to prepare chosen young men for the top positions, died partly as a result of the practice of directors bringing in youngsters recommended to their patronage.[23] Patronage was commonly a requirement for being granted an interview for even the lowlier type of post from which a man might set his sights on a management position. The Royal Exchange Assurance was not unusual in requiring a candidate for a clerkship to be nominated by one of the directors. In this company the practice lasted into the 1930s.[24] There were, too, the areas of business activity which were restricted to people with the right connections. Merchant banking, firms of stockbrokers, and Lloyds underwriters, for example, were open only 'by invitation'. The right connections might be family or friends, but it might also be the right school or university.

Patronage put family firms at no disadvantage where the owners were a successful business family with able sons, cousins, uncles, and sons-in-law. A few families produced at various times a number of sons of high managerial calibre – Cadburys, Courtaulds, and Sainsburys are amongst the best known. However, even the best families tended to run into barren times, and unless they could overcome their reluctance to recruit from outsiders, the firm had to struggle on with its inappropriate and/or ageing managers. After the family's talents had been exhausted, the family often turned to either the sons of friends and acquaintances or, particularly if the firm was experiencing financial difficulties, outsiders from an acceptable background who could bring much needed business skills to the firm. The men chosen were required not only to be useful to the firm, but sympathetic to its traditions – not always a good idea if the firm and the management were ailing. Lord Woolton, as an example, remembered the pained reaction in 1920 of the head of Lewis's (the stores group) when the vigorous Woolton joined the firm and pushed for changes to be made.[25]

Patronage, besides restricting the sources available to the firm of men with ability, had the further disadvantage that it could degenerate into nepotism. In all types of firm there was often no clear line between patronage, which could give a deserved uplift to a promising man, and nepotism which rewarded the inept. Both patronage and nepotism were widespread enough in British firms to be picked out as prominent characteristics in the making of British managers into the late 1930s – and both were criticised as major causes of business inefficiency. The economist, J. M. Keynes, was one of the many to argue in the inter-war period that 'hereditary influence in higher business appointments is one of the greatest dangers to efficiency in British business'. He saw that 'So many of our industries are now reaching a difficult age. They are becoming second and third generation businesses. They are getting into the hands of men who didn't create them and who couldn't possibly have created them.'[26] Nepotism was cited in 1942 as one of the three curses of British industry (the other two were secretiveness and traditionalism).[27] It was said even in the mid-1960s that 'Nepotism provides many ill-trained recruits for the boardrooms and managerial offices of the great public companies as well as for family businesses where it would be disingenuous to expect that its influence could ever be eliminated.'[28] A study of company

47

chairman in 1974 noted the persistence of a strong family influence into modern times among chairmen both in banking and in industry. 'Although the decline in family influence is quite clear', the study concluded, 'it appears to have been an important element in the careers of many chairmen of recent times. Approximately one quarter of those who became chairmen of major industrial and financial corporations in Britain after the Second World War had a family link wih the firm over which they presided.'[29] The electrical giant GEC was the prime post-war example of the costs of nepotism to a great public company. Lord Hirst had provided for his succession 'in an essentially dynastic way', and neither of the two men he named to follow him were up to the job. By 1960, GEC was 'an unprofitable dinosaur'.[30] Unfortunately for British industry, the lucky were not always the most able.

The UK firms which gave preference to new recruits from a particular school or university were not necessarily being unwise. In Japan the practice of recruiting potential managers only from a chosen university worked extremely well for the Japanese enterprise. However, there were differences in the two approaches which indicate that the practice did not work so well for the British. UK firms which gave preference to certain institutions usually chose those which had little understanding of, or even liking for, the business world. New recruits from the preferred public schools, and Oxford and Cambridge colleges, were emerging from an environment which valued success, but success preferably in the professions or government service; and in the arts rather than the sciences. In the public schools particularly, conformity was the key to success – and even to survival there.[31] Cambridge undergraduates were seen from a survey in 1959 to exhibit 'comparatively little taste for individualistic competition, and less than average liking for the responsibilities of leadership and organization'.[32]

The education the graduates had received had little bearing on a business career. Even where they had studied engineering, the sciences, law, or economics, the training was not geared to any extent to a business career. Some firms were satisfied with this approach (they, like the Japanese, preferred to choose the best material and train them over a long period of time within the company), but the University of Cambridge learned from a wide range of firms in the 1930s that the education it gave did not have industry sufficiently in mind. It was told, 'an engineer should be able to express himself readily on paper, by drawing as well as writing, but a Cambridge man who can make technical sketches is unusual, and one with any knowledge of draughtsmanship is an exception'.[33] Rolls Royce thought that too much time was spent at the university in laboratory work and not enough on the workshop side,[34] and Marconi found that physics students 'often have an inadequate knowledge of the practical use of electrical machines used in their laboratories'.[35] ICI found that the British chemists it recruited were much less commercially aware than their German or Swiss counterparts, and they needed training in the German language.[36] The graduates themselves were often aware that their university training had almost ignored the context in which their skills would be used. One young employee in ICI wrote to the Cambridge appointments board:

I do not think that those who are trained for business along technical lines are made sufficiently to realise that the sciences are applied in business wholly against a background of profit making. For example, when I read the Mechanical Sciences Tripos, in common with hundreds of others nearly all of whom were to go into the Engineering or allied trades, no reference whatsoever was made to costing, to commercial procedure or to economics pure or applied. We received no instruction about the place of the Engineering trade in the economic life of the country, or of British Engineering in relation to the World or its development. In the Chemistry Tripos I learned nothing whatsoever of applied chemistry, and left Cambridge in entire ignorance of the British Chemical Industry which I was to join for life. In fact I left Cambridge with the view that Science should be pursued for its own sake and that Business was a separate matter, rather obscure and not altogether respectable.[37]

Clearly the young in these institutions were hardly being prepared for a competitive business environment, yet the need to find employment for their growing numbers of students had persuaded these institutions from as early as the 1890s that they must press the claims of their men to business employers. The University of Cambridge appointments board had been exceptionally effective in placing men who needed help to find work, and about one-third of all Cambridge graduates were taking up business occupations (in this country and abroad) by 1939.[38] It has to be said, however, that not all of these men, despite their favourable start in life, found themselves in easy jobs with an open route to the Board. In the inter-war period Cambridge arts graduates became store assistants, Coca-Cola salesmen, commission-only insurance salesmen, and tea-shop under-managers, not only BBC announcers and ICI management trainees. Cambridge technical men could find themselves having to spend up to three years in a pupillage scheme of some kind before they could start to earn other than a nominal wage. They also had to accept that work in industry gave them a much lower status than work outside it, and even within industry their status was beneath that of the men on the non-technical side.

Until the late 1950s, the low status of business, combined with the growing numbers of young people needing to find employment in it, produced too many reluctant businessmen from the favoured institutions. Business was often a last resort for them, not their first.[39] This was not without its consequences. There was little chance after the first few years of employment of a man moving out of business (although some graduates managed to transfer to teaching), so that unless the company was able to do a good job of re-socialising, the reluctant recruit had two choices. He could just continue to do his job without much interest, or he could make his job and his environment more to his liking – more unbusinesslike, in fact.[40] The second choice seems to have been as common as the first, and when such men were in the majority in management the choice could have far-reaching effects on the company. There was, for example, a deliberate and much-lauded gentlemen's club atmosphere in the boardroom of Courtauld's between the 1930s and the 1950s. The atmosphere, according to the proud chairman, permeated the business – a business which the Board of predominantly public school men was slowly, but surely, leading downhill. The chairman who presided in the 1950s 'knew little or nothing about production technology, despised technical men, remained ignorant of science, and wholly indifferent to industrial relations'.[41] The Oxford college environment of ICI's Alkali Group ensured that the much-needed engineers and commercial men were kept in their place – well beneath the chemists, the lawyers, and the accountants.[42] The ICI men in the post-1945 period considered themselves, with some justification, as something of an elite, but 'they do not necessarily regard themselves as being an elite of business'.[43]

However, most British firms did not get their future management material from the public schools or the universities, old or new. British managers and directors were not commonly from the highest level of the education system in the nineteenth century, and neither were they in the first half of the twentieth. As late as the mid-1950s less than half of the directors and around one in five managers (one in three top managers) of large British firms were graduates.[44] Germany, Japan, and the US had surpassed this in the 1920s, yet systematic entry into UK business from the universities was hardly known before the 1930s. There were large firms in the motor industry still not recruiting engineering graduates in the mid-1950s – when the high import tariff on foreign cars and components had started to come down. This was not restricted to manufacturing industry. Two large service industries (banking and insurance), for example, did not normally recruit from the universities until the mid-1950s. Potential recruits were advised in the mid-1930s that a few banks took on university graduates 'in special instances', but the graduates were in no way special recruits. They spent the first few years, as did all the junior clerks, on routine work, studying in their own time for the Institute of Bankers' examinations. After this period of probation, and provided they passed the examinations, they were considered, with all other clerks, for the few posts of higher responsibility. Insurance companies recruited graduates occasionally for a statistical or actuarial post. There were by the mid-1950s some 400,000 to 450,000 managers in UK firms, needing a recruitment of some 14,000 men annually.[45] The universities supplied the whole of industry and commerce combined with less than 5,000 people annually (roughly a third each of arts men, scientists, and technologists).[46]

Very few of these had had any introduction to business methods or techniques. Some universities offered industrial management, or at least cost accounting, to their technical men and this increased considerably after the Second World War, but it was still an extraneous part of their technical training not an integral part which affected their approach to their work. Commerce graduates, and to a lesser extent, economics graduates went into industry, and some men from non-business disciplines added a management course to their education, but the numbers were very small – they were still in their hundreds in the 1950s, not thousands. The annual production of commerce and business studies graduates had reached 437, out of some 36,000 graduates of all kinds, by the 1960s.[47]

British firms in fact had continued to take most of the young men who would become managers from the lower levels of the education system, as they had done before the 'scientific revolution' of the late nineteenth century. British managers and directors began their careers as school-leavers rather than college graduates. Firms recruited boys from the State schools at fourteen, then fifteen, then sixteen years of age. Recruits from the private schools tended to be older. Only when the supply of school-leavers began to look uncertain in the 1930s and more of the brighter lads were thought to be going into higher education, did large firms begin recruiting from higher education in any systematic way.

New recruits into industry entered with only minimal levels of either general or vocational education, thus the major part of the burden of preparation for a business career was still to be tackled when the education system let the young people go. New recruits looked to industry to indicate how they could best prepare themselves for a career in management; what knowledge and educational qualifications they should aim for.

Industry, however, normally gave little indication to either new recruits or existing employees on how they could use education to advance their ambitions. Employers saw the issue as an employee, not a management, problem. It was for the employee to ensure that he had prepared himself with the necessary general and vocational education sufficient to fit him for the post he aimed for. There was rarely any direct pressure on employees to increase their understanding of their work through formal education. In the 1930s the banks began to want men looking for promotion to take the Institute of Bankers' examinations, the railway companies those of the Institute of Transport, and large manufacturers had begun to indicate by the 1930s that certain formal technical qualifications were now expected, but otherwise men studied if they wished and what they wished.

The only realistic method of continuing education available to interested employees was after-work study. The technical schools offered a plethora of courses and qualifications (the jungle of qualifications then, as now, making an informed choice very difficult), and the civic universities offered a wide range of below degree-level courses, and degree work, for both technical and commercial men. Many offered courses leading to the qualifications of the professional institutes. There had been an enormous increase in the number of small professional bodies from the late nineteenth century offering their own qualifications in individual areas of business expertise.[48] Young employees turned to these not only for vocational education but to acquire a formal, portable, qualification. They studied for them outside of working hours – via correspondence courses, or evening classes in schools, technical colleges, and universities. There were undoubted advantages to the firm of this approach to business education. The men were demonstrating initiative and a willingness to study in their own time. Since firms were not in the habit of increasing the salary of those passing the examinations, the practice cost them nothing. There was some move towards helping with the time needed for study and examinations, but it had not gone far even into the 1950s. The banks which preferred men to take the relevant examinations began in 1936 to give their employees half a day off work at examination time. There was no improvement on this until the 1950s.[49]

But there were also disadvantages to the firm in allowing the content and standard of the vocational education of their potential managers to be controlled entirely by a multitude of autonomous professional bodies. The professional examinations offered a limited and narrow type of education and this encouraged in the men a limited and specialist outlook inside the firm.

The professional associations, after the first few years of their existence, had become primarily examining bodies. Much of their work involved the setting and marking of examination papers. The advancement of the subject itself and the wider business education of their members formed only a small part of their activities. A number of associations did begin to include in their examination syllabuses subjects which they considered useful to their members as potential managers – for example, the Works Management Association, the Office Management Association, and the Purchasing Officers Association, included by 1939 such subjects as business organisation, accounting and costing, business statistics, industrial history, economics, and industrial and commercial law.[50] But the membership of such bodies was very small – 800, 600, and 500 for those listed – and they were not joined by the larger and more prestigious accountancy bodies. The primary interest of the professional bodies lay in the status of their subject and the status of their own association: they were not therefore interested in embracing other subjects and certainly not the lower-status branches of their own subject. The Chartered Accountants, for example, shunned the Cost Accountants – who set up their own professional association in response in 1919. Because the controlling bodies of the professional associations were fearful of a takeover by the education system, and because they were composed of practical men, they kept an arm's-length approach to the work going on in the colleges and universities, especially in the important area of accountancy.

The accounting bodies, whose members had become increasingly necessary to British firms from the 1890s, first for audit work and taxation and then for wider financial advice, did not themselves make much provision for the education of their candidates, so that the great majority even in the late 1950s were taking correspondence courses.[51] The competing accountancy groups were able to ensure that their perceived needs, which were not necessarily those of the firm, were met in the course content. Their members gained their professional qualifications still, in business terms, semi-literate. The narrowness of the education of accountants, in terms of their own specialism as well as in the wider context of business management, was continually pointed out to the governing bodies. But these bodies saw no need for radical change: on their own terms they were undoubtedly very successful.

Inside the firm this narrow outlook and identification with an outside profession also reinforced the tendency towards compartmentalism, long characteristic of British firms. This compartmentalism arose, firstly, from the horizontal divide which commonly existed between the men and management, and between the levels of management. Promotion into management was understood in many firms by both men and management as being a transfer of loyalty from one side to the other. There was, secondly, the vertical divide between departments. It was not unusual in large British firms for the managers in one department to have little idea of, or sympathy for, what the other departments were doing. A wider understanding of the enterprise had not been part of their on-the-job training, and senior managers, whose function it was to ensure overall control and co-ordination, typically spent their time on the day-to-day activities of running a single department or function.

As the specialist moved to the top of the promotion ladder, the narrowness of his education became more of a drawback. Senior managers advise on the allocation of the firm's resources of men, money, methods, materials, and machinery for the provision of goods and services to a market. They also take calculated risks for the future. Yet the professional education offered by the associations gave little more than some expertise in not more than one of these areas. The accountants had acquired a reputation for understanding the wider problems of the firm and they became more numerous and influential as managers, yet even they dealt primarily with money; they had been trained to avoid risks, and to concentrate their attention on figures which described what had happened in the past rather than with figures as a form of management control and an aid to decision-making for future projects.[52]

However, an aspiring manager could, with difficulty, equip himself with formal educational qualifications appropriate to the area of business he had chosen. He also needed opportunities to gain experience. This was easier for a favoured few for whom a special effort would be made. Heirs apparent (or 'crown princes') were usually given opportunities for training within the firm and the early exercise of responsibility. They would expect to be a member of management, or a director of the firm, by their mid-twenties. A sample of such men in the 1950s, however, found that even for this favoured group the experiences had not been very varied. Few had worked outside of the family firm, or had spent much time in functions other than production and sales.[53] There was another favoured group, the 'special entrants', that is, those men with no special abilities but with influence, and these too might expect opportunities to be put their way. There was a small number of graduate management trainees who might expect to be given sufficient training to allow them to arrive at the first rung of management by their mid-twenties. There were also the specially chosen individuals, like those graduates who were picked out from their colleges to be a successor to the managing director, or 'with the Board in view', or for general management. Occasionally, a business leader would pick out a young member of staff to be his personal assistant and groom him for early responsibility –

as did Hugo Hirst of GEC throughout the inter-war period and Marcus Sieff of Marks and Spencer from the late 1950s. For all these groups a special effort might be made. But for the majority of managers, and potential managers, in British firms, there were few opportunities for experience-based learning, that is, for widening their experience by movement into other departments and deepening their understanding under the guidance of an effective manager, although there were many years of straight repetition.

There was usually some opportunity for a new recruit of any kind to move around inside the firm during his early years. He could ask to be moved to another department or even a different function if he wanted to gain more experience. But, once he began to acquire expertise in one function, and perhaps to study for membership of a relevant professional body, he normally remained in that function for the duration of his career.[54] When there was a promotion to be made, the choice was normally made from amongst those within the department. What was looked for was a man with the proven specialist ability to do the job on offer, who would fit in, and who deserved it. If there was no suitable man with a sufficient level of specialist skills and acceptable attitude and appearance, then a good specialist from outside the firm was the second best choice. A candidate from another function looking for wider experience was not an acceptable option. Thus in Britain sales representatives became sales managers, sales managers became marketing directors; finance directors were promoted accountants. It was unusual for an accountant to have had any significant experience in buying or sales, and it was most unusual for either an accountant or buyer to have worked on the production side. A number of surveys on managers and directors, whose careers had begun in the inter-war period, appeared in the UK after the Second World War and these give a good idea of the extent of the narrow experience of managers, both within the firm and between firms. A survey of over 3,000 managers in the 1950s found that not only was a change of function extremely rare (only some 13 per cent of the sample had changed function), but even a change of department was comparatively rare.[55] A massive 61 per cent had experienced neither a change of function nor a change of department. Other surveys had similar findings. Neither had the managers gained a wider experience from other firms. The surveys showed that over 40 per cent had made not even one change of company. Forty-four per cent of the top managers in one sample had spent all their working lives in the one company. In a sample of over 1,000 directors in 1955, 41 per cent had remained in the same company and a further 31 per cent had made only one change.[56] In a 1969 survey of 120 top businessmen, 46 per cent had made no change.[57]

If a man did move across to another firm for more opportunities to exercise responsibility and gain authority, he might not increase his chances very much since his new firm would also place him inside a specialism, and there he would stay.

In some functions a man could move up somewhat faster and higher than in others, so that where he started off was important. Generally the financial and commercial side of the firm took men quicker into senior management and the Board; production and personnel had a cut-off point below the Board and there were fewer senior jobs available in these areas. Engineers and chemists could get to the Board, but they were not normally on the fastest route to the top. Qualified chemists and engineers were notable for their absence from British boardrooms. The more influence a man had, the wider choice of function he was likely to have, and the less likely he was to choose production. The elementary school recruit was generally to be found there.

The level at which a man started in the firm could be as influential to his chances of reaching management as the function he made his career in. Even in firms where the route from the bottom to the top of the managerial hierarchy was relatively open, a man starting at the very bottom either on the commercial or the technical side would have few opportunities for promotion. In 1920, it was estimated that in firms with between 300 and 800 clerks, prospects for the rank and file were no brighter than those for factory workers; only one in ten had any chance of rising to departmental or sectional head.[58] On the technical side, a survey in the 1950s found that ex-trade apprentices often took twenty years to reach the ranks of management.

An option open to firms was to create opportunities for good men to experience responsibilities commensurate with their capabilities. However, created opportunities for numbers of men had of necessity to be part of a larger scheme of planning for management, and, with few exceptions, schemes designed to prepare numbers of men for management were not part of the British experience. Unilever, one company which was noted for its strong emphasis on offering good men wide experience and increasing levels of responsibility in various parts of its empire, was 50 per cent Dutch owned. The practices which brought men to the top in British firms were of a much looser type.

British firms did not construct a definite system for seeking out and developing the potential talent in their employ. They did not trawl for talent in any systematic way. There were several well-understood methods of assisting talent-spotting – internal advertisements, merit rating and annual assessments, interviewing, and encouraging managers to accept it as a responsibility – but few firms by the late 1950s had yet decided to use them to any extent.[59] Promotion policies were not sophisticated. An enquiry in the late 1920s found that only a small minority of larger establishments had 'any definite and organised system of promotion',[60] and there was no surge towards one until after the Second World War. As a general rule, and apart from those with influence, the immediate superior made his recommendations for the vacancy based on his knowledge and his preferences, and usually this was sufficient. Personnel records and appointment committees, which would have allowed a more thorough assessment by a wider group of people, perhaps looking at the longer-term potential of the candidates, remained comparatively rare.

A number of large firms in the late 1920s did decide that the British way of producing managers was not providing the quality of man they wanted, in the numbers they wanted. The 1920s had seen a marked growth – by merger and internal expansion – in the scale of industrial and commercial undertakings, demanding larger investments in capital-intensive plant and stronger forms of managerial control.[61] Firms were also beginning to feel the lack of recruitment, and the loss of staff, during the First World War. Business conditions were also looking better after the mid-1920s for much of manufacturing industry: manufacturing output grew fairly rapidly between 1924 and 1929.[62]

Specialists were slowly moving in to take over part of the burden from the old-style managements, but some of the largest manufacturing firms decided that they would take active steps to provide the organisation with supplies of higher managerial ability. Some of these firms were trying to make up in a hurry for previous neglect. This was not an unusual problem from the mid-1920s onwards. Pilkington Brothers found in the late 1920s that it had acute management problems, and the advanced age of the current directors forced the firm to look outside for young men with ability. Courtaulds in the 1940s found itself with a shortage of potential directors in the right age-group and too few able middle managers – due in part to the inadequacies of pre-war recruitment. Lord Trent, on his retirement in 1954 from the chairmanship of Boots, had made no provision for a successor. In United Steel, by 1950 there was a gap in middle management and too few younger men on the Board.

The firms which had decided to act to improve the supply of men capable of joining the ranks of management understood their need to be not for more specialists and not for the average man, which they had in abundance, but for men with the potential for general management, which they saw in terms of initiating, controlling, and directing operations, rather than merely supporting existing systems. Trawling for men with high potential in their own companies, or choosing men for training from amongst their own specialists, seemed a longer and less certain way of finding the wanted recruits than bringing in new men who had been picked out as having the qualities needed. The qualities they sought lay almost exclusively in the area of personality. They did not seek a high level of general and vocational education, as happened in Germany, or high academic abilities and correct attitudes to business, as in Japan.

British firms decided that what they wanted was men with characteristics which contrasted with those of the specialist – broad vision, no specialist training, an ability to communicate. They demanded, in particular, men with what they referred to as 'leadership qualities'. There was a widespread belief in the transferability of an ability to lead: a man who could lead his team to victory on the rugby field was the man who could lead the workers to greater effort in the workplace. A well-researched report to the University of Cambridge appointments board judged that the type of man wanted by British firms looking for managers, was one

with a wide outlook, a sense of fairness towards others, a capacity to take responsibility and show initiative and to devote himself to his work. The 'bookish' type of man is not looked upon with favour and is considered inferior to the man who has taken part in the sporting and social life of the university.[63]

The appointments boards at both Oxford and Cambridge universities seem to have had little difficulty in understanding what it was that firms were looking for, even if they could not always supply it. The man with the right characteristics need not necessarily, however, have been to a university. Cambridge decided that industrialists 'want people of a particular type and they find the university a fruitful source of supply, but it is the type they want, not the university man as such, and provided they get the right type they are prepared to recruit from any source'.[64]

In the late 1920s ICI (along with many other firms) went to the public schools for suitable candidates. The company came to an arrangement with a few top schools whereby chosen boys would be recruited and treated as potential managers. But the scheme did not work well, and it was soon dropped (see Chapter 4). ICI, and other firms, then went to Cambridge and Oxford universities for the older version of the type they were looking for. They expected to find him in the arts graduate, and preferred to restrict their search to arts men.

The technical man was not generally regarded as a potential candidate for business management. The science or technology graduate was believed to have been exposed to an educational experience which was not likely to produce the right type to lead British industry. Businessmen argued that the technical man's heavy programme of work as an undergraduate had allowed him little time to develop either his personality or interests in subjects outside his own discipline. They complained that this heavy programme was an intensely specialised one, leading to a tunnel vision which was not appropriate in management. There was widespread support for these views. It was often said of young men who had studied the sciences that their general education was weak. A government committee in the early 1930s remarked that 'Our witnesses view with anxiety the prospect of a growing race of illiterate scientists unable to express themselves adequately or intelligently in their own language, and ignorant alike of history and of the forces other than the chemical and physical which make the world in which they live.'[65] The highly trained technologist was often accused not only of being ignorant of the principles of industrial organisation and management, but of showing no inclination to accept administrative responsibility.[66]

There was some justification for these complaints. A higher

technical education in England demanded (and still demands) specialisation at a very early age – usually between thirteen and fifteen years. This is much earlier than that expected of young people abroad. A technical education also demanded a degree of separation from non-science disciplines which could have benefited neither the technical nor the arts man. But while businessmen had strong support for their criticisms of the over-specialised education of such men, the business argument that the scientist's formal education unfitted him for business management relied heavily on the fact that business did not offer a programme of education and experience designed to widen his understanding. Nor did business show to education that a good position was possible for the scientist with a broader education. The technical man, and particularly the engineer from a new university, knew that he had to find work on the basis of his technical achievements (and any influence he could muster), not his knowledge of non-technical subjects.

British industry continued to be criticised throughout the first half of the twentieth century for not investing directly in management on a much larger scale. The increasing level of intervention from the mid-1920s in the usual processes which produced managers did little to raise the standard of the management stock available to British industry. Government reports continued to identify failings in British firms in costing systems, marketing skills, knowledge of foreign languages, quality of design, and production techniques. Making managers the British way had produced for the country an industrial leadership less well educated and less widely experienced than their counterparts abroad.

This is not to suggest that good managers did not emerge. There *were* good training firms; men continued to found their own companies, and the practices that were common throughout British business were not totally inimicable to good men appearing at the top. They were not, however, designed to assist good men to appear, and the difficulties they presented proved too formidable for many potentially good recruits. The British way was inefficient and wasteful. Employers continued to prefer, however, to work within these traditional practices rather than make radical change. The following chapters will show that they were not prepared to allow education to make a much larger contribution to the making of the nation's managers.

References

1 E. J. Hobsbawm, *The Age of Revolution 1789–1848*, Mentor Books, New York, 1962, p. 48.

2 Hobsbawm, *The Age*, p. 54.

3 P. Mathias, *The First Industrial Nation: An Economic History of Britain 1700–1914*, Methuen, 1969, p. 158.

4 Hobsbawm, *The Age*, p. 47.

5 *Journal of the Chemical Society*, XXXI, 1877, p. 493.

6 In Hobsbawm, *The Age*, p. 48.

7 W. H. G. Armytage, *Civic Universities*, Ernest Benn, 1955, p. 233.

8 C. Trebilcock, *The Vickers Brothers: Armaments and Enterprise 1854–1914*, Europa Press, 1977, p. 127.

9 S. Rothblatt, *Tradition and Change in English Liberal Education*, Faber and Faber, 1976, p. 166.

10 *Educational Times*, 1 December 1887.

11 A. D. Chandler, Jr, *Scale and Scope: the Dynamics of Industrial Capitalism*, Harvard University Press, Cambridge, MA, 1990, p. 268.

12 Management Research Groups (MRGs), Labour Section meeting 15 January 1931, ref. 12/474, available in LSE library.

13 Chandler, *Scale and Scope*, p. 240.

14 Chandler, *Scale and Scope*, p. 240.

15 S. Melman, *Dynamic Factors in Industrial Productivity*, Basil Blackwell, Oxford, 1956, p. 85.

16 D. F. Channon, *The Strategy and Structure of British Enterprise*, Macmillan, 1973, p. 75.

17 D. J. Richardson, 'The history of J. Lyons & Co. Ltd.', unpublished, undated typescript, kindly loaned by the author, p. 527.

18 W. J. Reader, *A House in the City: A Study of the City and of the Stock Exchange Based on the Records of Foster & Braithwaite 1825–1975*, B. T. Batsford, 1979, pp. 179–81.

19 G. Turner, *Business in Britain*, Penguin ed., 1971, p. 246.

20 R. Lewis and R. Stewart, *The Boss: The Life and Times of the British Business Man*, J. M. Dent, 1963, p. 99.

21 Federation of British Industries (FBI), Education Committee Memorandum on Education, January 1918, p. 8, PRO ref. ED24/657.

22 *Britain's Industrial Future, being the Report of the Liberal Industrial Inquiry*, Ernest Benn, 1928, p. 90.

23 University of Cambridge Appointments Board (UCAB), Employers' Visits, 13 January 1931, ref. APTB 10.2.

24 B. Supple, *The Royal Exchange Assurance*, Cambridge University Press, Cambridge, 1970, p. 390.

25 Lord Woolton, *The Memoirs of The Rt. Hon. The Earl of*

Woolton, Cassell, 1959, p. 74.

26 In D. Moggridge, ed., *J. M. Keynes: Activities 1922–1929: the Return to Gold and Industrial Policy*, X1X, part 11, Cambridge University Press, Cambridge, 1981, p. 652.

27 Institute of Industrial Administration (IIA), *Journal*, IV, 4 (new series), September 1942, p. 12.

28 G. C. Allen, *The Structure of Industry in Britain: A Study in Economic Change*, Longmans, 1967, p. 190.

29 P. Stanworth and A. Giddens, eds., *Elites and Power in British Society*, Cambridge University Press, Cambridge, 1974, p. 91.

30 R. Jones and O. Marriott, *Anatomy of a Merger: A History of G.E.C., A.E.I., and English Electric*, Jonathan Cape, 1970, p. 206.

31 J. Rae, *The Public School Revolution 1964–1979*, Faber and Faber, 1981, p. 96.

32 M. Abrams, 'Business aspirants from universities', *The Manager*, September 1961, p. 721.

33 UCAB, Firms' Replies, 9 November 1938, ref. APTB 14/13.

34 UCAB, Firms' Replies, 1 November 1938, ref. APTB 14/13.

35 UCAB, Firms' Replies, 31 October 1938, ref. APTB 14/13.

36 ICI, 'Conference on Training of Chemists for Industry', File CR/215/7/- 1926–9, Box 457.

37 UCAB, Graduates' Replies, 2 May 1939, ref. APTB 14/14.

38 (Spens) Report, *University Education and Business*, Cambridge University Press, Cambridge, 1945, p. 26.

39 Spens, *University Education*, p. 17.

40 Abrams, 'Business aspirants', p. 721.

41 D. C. Coleman, *Courtaulds: An Economic and Social History: Crisis and Change 1940–1965*, III, Clarendon Press, Oxford, 1980, p. 23.

42 W. J. Reader, *Imperial Chemical Industries: A History: The First Quarter-Century 1926–1952*, II, Oxford University Press, Oxford, 1975, p. 71.

43 Turner, *Business in Britain*, p. 142.

44 Acton Society Trust (AST), *Management Succession: The Recruitment, Selection, Training and Promotion of Managers*, AST, 1956, p. 8.

45 Political and Economic Planning (PEP), *Manpower*, PEP, 1949.

46 Political and Economic Planning (PEP), 'Graduates' jobs', *Planning*, XXI, 24 October 1955, p. 198.

47 R. Lynn, *The Universities and the Business Community*, Industrial Educational and Research Foundation, Occasional Paper 6, 1969, p. 12.

48 G. Millerson, *The Qualifying Associations: A Study in Profes-sionalization*, Routledge and Kegan Paul, 1964.

49 E. Green, *Debtors to their Profession: A History of the Institute of Bankers, 1879–1979*, Methuen, 1979, p. 155.

50 R. Pugh, ed., *British Management Year Book*, 1939, p. 121.

51 A. Plant, 'Universities and the making of businessmen', in D. Grant, ed., *The University and Business*, University of Toronto Press, Toronto, 1958, p. 524.

52 N. A. H. Stacey, *English Accountancy 1800–1954*, Gee and Co., 1954.

53 R. V. Clements, *Managers: A Study of Their Careers in Industry*, George Allen and Unwin, 1958, p. 34.

54 D. Granick, *Managerial Comparisons of Four Developed Countries: France, Britain, United States, and Russia*, MIT Press, Cambridge, MA, 1972, p. 57, and Clements, *Managers*, p. 107.

55 AST, *Management Succession*, p. 13.

56 G. H. Copeman, *Leaders of British Industry*, Gee and Co., 1955, p. 107.

57 D. J. Hall and G. Amado-Fischgrund, 'Chief Executives in Britain', *European Business*, January 1969, p. 46.

58 *Business Organisation and Management*, I, March 1920, p. 55.

59 AST, *Management Succession*, pp. 38f.

60 *Britain's Industrial Future*, p. 131.

61 For details of this merger wave, see L. Hannah, *The Rise of the Corporate Economy*, Methuen, 1979 ed., ch. 7.

62 R. C. O. Matthews, C. H. Feinstein, and J. C. Odling-Smee, *British Economic Growth 1856–1973*, Clarendon Press, Oxford, 1982, p. 383.

63 Spens, *University Education*, p. 40.

64 Spens, *University Education*, p. 34.

65 In H. T. Tizard, 'Science at the universities', *Report of the British Association for the Advancement of Science*, 1934, p. 217.

66 (Percy) Report, *Higher Technological Education*, Ministry of Education, HMSO, 1945, p. 22.

Chapter 4

The British rejection of formal education

There has been a good deal of support for the idea that the British education system failed British industry, hence the low level of educational qualifications amongst its managers. It is undoubtedly true that in the period under review, from 1890 to 1960, education at any level had not geared its teaching or socialised its students towards the industrial world nearly to the extent that happened abroad. British industry could rightly complain of an anti-industry bias in a system which placed a career in industry below a career in almost anything else. In addition, the number of university graduates being produced for selection was, until the expansion of the 1960s, very small. There were only 20,000 full-time students in 1900 (0.8 per cent of the age group), 42,000 in 1924 (1.5 per cent), 50,000 in 1938 (1.7 per cent), and 100,000 in 1960 (4.0 per cent).[1] This was proportionately rather fewer than in Germany and markedly fewer than in the US. And no-one could doubt the widespread ignorance of industrial affairs in schools and colleges. However, too much sympathy would be misplaced. The gap between industry and education could have been very much narrower, and education much more useful to industry, if industry had wanted it. But industry showed time and again that it had no interest in a closer relationship. British businessmen constantly said no to the efforts being made, by government, educationalists and some businessmen, to provide higher levels of general, technical, and business education for industry's use.

Manufacturing industry, in particular, placed a firmly restraining hand on all attempts to raise the general education of the young through longer years of compulsory schooling. In 1918 the country was asked to accept proposals which, if accepted, would have constituted a major advance in the general education of young people. The Fisher Education Bill had not only recommended raising the compulsory school-leaving age from twelve to fourteen years for all children, but extending their education part-time until the age of eighteen (following the German example). Those in paid employment would have to be released to attend classes. Industrialists were prominent amongst those who thought that the country was not ready to begin such an advance, and would not be ready for the foreseeable future, on the grounds of cost. The compulsory and free 'continuation classes', of up to eight hours a week, met with strong resistance from industrialists (and others, who had their own preferences).

The new Federation of British Industries (FBI), some of whose leaders were enthusiastic supporters of education, circulated its members for their views. Of the 2,044 who replied only twenty-three were in favour of part-time education for all in the age group.[2] The clear preference was for any extra resources to be concentrated on a selected few. Just over half approved the proposal for increasing the number of secondary-school places. The FBI, therefore, decided to recommend this to Fisher, along with certain suggestions for elementary education. The 'less promising children', that is, those who were not chosen for secondary education at twelve years of age and who could not afford to buy a place in a secondary school,

should continue in the Elementary School until the end of the school period in which they attain the age of 14, receiving, however, during these last two years a more general training calculated rather to develop their character, general intelligence, and powers of observation than to increase their knowledge of educational subjects. Part of this training might be directly vocational and intended to fit the child for the particular industry which it will enter at 14. This would apply more especially to towns and districts which are almost exclusively engaged in one industry.

Thus, for over 90 per cent of the nation's young, elementary education would continue to be completed at twelve years of age: on this would be built a vocational training sufficient to prepare children for the local industry. There was, however, no indication that this vocational education would be recognised by local employers or that it could lead on to a vocational qualification. Industrialists knew that their recommendations would leave British education for juveniles far behind that in other countries: in America there were 148 per 10,000 undergoing education after fourteen years of age, in Scandinavian countries ninety-six, but in England only twenty.

The Fisher Act did empower local authorities to enforce day continuation tuition for certain youths between fourteen and sixteen years of age, but where they tried to do so, 'they met the opposition of employers who refused to take on youngsters from such areas'.[3] After the cutbacks in 1920, local authorities could not afford to keep their initiatives going and government no longer expected the provision to be made. While some authorities offered voluntary continuation schooling, the major advance of part-time, post-school education for all was effectively dead by 1924. When the idea was raised again in the late 1920s, business opposition was again strong. A government committee in 1928 was advised that 'employers collectively are as much opposed to the institution of Day Continuation Schools as to the raising of the school leaving age'.[4] The idea failed again in the 1930s and the 1940s. The failure to develop continuation schooling meant that the gap which existed between the low level of general education most children received and that needed to begin any form of technical education was a continuing drawback. It has been deemed by Sanderson 'a major lost opportunity of the twentieth century', since

The avoidance of an abrupt break between school and work and the interleaving of both activities for teenagers was an important element in the formation of the educated and adaptable German workforce in the nineteenth century. It would also have been especially valuable in England with so limited a system of secondary education for the working classes.[5]

There were firms which had reacted differently. Even before Fisher, some firms provided educational facilities for their young employees. The Fisher Committee had details of thirty-one such firms, and many of these agreed to adjust their schemes to meet the requirements of the Fisher Act. The FBI had seen no real place for a Works School in the Fisher Act,[6] but Tootal, Broadhurst and Lee (textiles) had set up its school at Bolton, 'dissenting from the majority report of a Committee of the Federation of British Industries on the practicability of day continuation schools'.[7] A few others – including Reckitt and Sons (laundry products), Cadbury (chocolate), Cable and Wireless (communications), and C. and J. Clark (shoes) – set up their own schools. In 1930, thirteen firms were known to be contributing in some way to this type of venture.[8] The facilities of Cadbury's day continuation school were open to any other Birmingham firm; but in 1935 only two were sending their young employees.

The proposal to raise the school-leaving age to fourteen was put into effect in 1922 (with some concession to the textile industry, which continued to employ twelve-year-olds, as 'half-timers'). It stayed at fourteen years throughout the 1930s, the worst years of juvenile unemployment. The FBI had made it plain in 1925 that industry would not agree to its being raised further.[9] In 1928 another employers' group, the National Confederation of Employers' Organisations, had argued that the great mass of employers would be opposed to the raising of the school-leaving age, on the grounds of cost and the shortage of juvenile labour.[10] It was finally raised to fifteen years in 1947, and to sixteen years in 1972.

Industrialists had resisted the calls for longer general education on many counts. They were sensitive to any waste of resources in over-educating people for the job they had to do. The FBI Education Committee felt compelled to advise the Fisher committee that 'in selecting children for higher education care should be taken to avoid creating, as was done, for example, in India, a large class of persons, whose education is unsuitable for the employment which they eventually enter'.[11] In 1920 it wrote again to Fisher on the same theme. 'In the interests of the country, it is undesirable to allow young persons to waste years at the public expense on an education which does not improve their value as a national asset.'[12] British industrialists, moreover, greatly objected to contributing even more funds to a service which gave so little promise of an economic return: the most enthusiastic supporters could not point to a direct economic benefit to firms of this extra schooling. Firms like Rowntree and Cadbury could only argue that their educational programmes gave them a wider and better choice of young worker, not necessarily improved productivity. Most employers put education under the heading 'welfare', and welfare was only afforded when times were very good. Too many young people, they believed, would not benefit from more education, particularly compulsory education after they had left school and for which wages would be reduced. Employers were, moreover, alive to the fact that longer years of schooling might lessen the normally ample supplies of juvenile labour for the factories, and that better educated youngsters tended to look for white-collar rather than factory work.

Although formal technical education might have been thought to have been more obviously of value to industrial activity, British businessmen demonstrated a similar lack of enthusiasm for this area of education. There had been a great extension of technical instruction in the last quarter of the nineteenth century. There were full-time trade schools and junior technical schools, and part-time day and evening classes for those in employment. There were classes in most large towns to prepare young people for the (trade) examinations of the City and Guilds Institute and a wide range of other examinations in vocational subjects. It was hoped that the working classes, for whom technical instruction was seen to be particularly appropriate, would take full advantage of what was available to them.

Individual businessmen had been amongst the most enthusiastic promoters of technical institutes and technical instruction. However, the demand for this great expansion had not come from industry, and the movement had received 'little blessing or guidance from the manufacturing and business community'.[13] A survey of industrialists' views in 1910 on the benefits to be derived from the technical facilities concluded that 'They think that evening schools, technical institutes, and schools of art may help the individual pupil; it does not enter their minds that such schools might aid their industries.'[14] Manchester's Owens College offered as early as 1907 to set up a scheme of apprenticeship training to help the engineering firms in the area but 'there was no weight of opinion behind the movement'. The Manchester Chamber of Commerce, itself in favour of better educational facilities, found that many of the engineering employers 'take no interest whatever in the training and education of their apprentices. Others object to assisting a process which they fear may some day produce a man capable of ousting them from their position or of becoming a competitor in business.'[15] Industries which depended directly on technical skills were no more likely to give technical education active support than those less involved. Most engineering training continued in much the same way – a laborious apprenticeship in the workshops – as it had done fifty years earlier.[16] Neither shipbuilding nor marine engineering were persuaded that they should improve their support. Before the First World War, it has been argued, the employers in these industries could not see the value of applied science and technical instruction to their industries, and after the First World War they were not willing to put their own money into it.[17]

Technical education became more widespread over the decades, although in the 1930s the demand for instruction in the technical colleges still came primarily from employees, not employers.[18] Day-release from firms, for example, covered about 1.5 per cent of the occupied population under eighteen years of age in the early 1930s,[19] and just over 2 per cent (42,000 out of two million) by the Second World War.[20] It did increase markedly after the war – to 27 per cent of boys and 7 per cent of girls by 1954–55.[21] The increase, however, did not demonstrate to contemporaries that technical education had yet been taken up with enthusiasm. It was

still abundantly clear that the support is frequently given not so much from inner conviction as under duress of circumstance, the most powerful factor being the acute shortage of manpower. Business firms know well enough that further training by day-release is as attractive as good wages to parents and head teachers interested in placing young people in employment.[22]

Most British employers had continued to prefer that their young people, if they wanted to take vocational examinations, took them in their own time and at their own expense.

British businessmen also rejected the claims of the universities to be an indispensable source of expertise and manpower. In the late nineteenth century, when their major foreign competitors had begun to look to the colleges to provide them with men with engineering or business skills, British firms were not persuaded that they needed what the colleges could offer. They saw little need in their own firms for men with a higher level of theoretical knowledge and mental training than that already available to them, and there was no shortage of men of the type which had traditionally manned British firms. Such men learned their skills through practical experience, which businessmen much preferred, and there were facilities for employees to improve their general and technical education if they needed to. Firms could rely on outside consultants and other agencies, particularly from the universities, to provide them with any special needs that could not be met by men within the firm. The numbers of university graduates being recruited into British firms did grow over the decades, and the pace quickened from the 1930s. The larger intake resulted, however, from the larger numbers of graduates needing employment; from the tightening of the market for able school-leavers; the efforts of the universities to place their men in business positions; the search of large manufacturing firms for men with personality, and only then from a rising demand for men who had experienced a university education.

There *was* competition for graduates. Most university graduates in the late nineteenth century still went into the Church, law, medicine, education, government service and the Indian Civil Service. Then, with the expansion of the education system and the new arrangement for training teachers in university departments, teaching became a very important recruiter, of scientists as well as arts men. The majority of degree students up to 1914 were intending teachers: they had accepted free training and in return bound themselves to teach for seven years after they had gained their diploma. The graduates of the new 'redbrick' universities in the major trading centres were not more likely to be heading for a business career. The majority in each case went into teaching. In Manchester in 1906 47 per cent became teachers.[23] Teaching took the largest proportion of LSE students in the 1920s – only some 14 per cent went into industry. But in the 1930s the numbers entering industry began to rise, particularly from the University of Cambridge, which had sent a much higher proportion of its graduates into business both before and after the First World War. The proportion from Cambridge entering business firms of all kinds had risen to almost one-third of its output by the Second World War[24] (this does include the numbers going abroad for British firms). The proportion from all universities together was probably around 25 to 30 per cent in the late 1930s, of a total output of some 12,000. In 1950, according to the first multi-university survey of the first employment of university graduates, the recruitment of university men had reached almost 35 per cent, amounting to just under 5,000 males (around one-third each of arts men, scientists, and technologists).[25]

But while there had been competition, and the numbers entering industry had been very small until the 1930s, British firms had not been starved of graduates. The supply had in most years from the 1890s exceeded the demand. The records of the university appointments boards[26] confirm that, from the beginning of the scientific revolution and for the next sixty years, the normal employment prospects for graduates considering a business career (normal, that is, without the help of patronage or a period of economic boom) were generally poor. Before the First World War, at a time when criticism of British engineering firms was very strong, and 'Made in Germany' and 'The American Invaders' hysteria was being whipped up by the national press, the University of London appointments board found particular difficulty in placing its engineering graduates in industry. In 1914, with the chemical industry clearly losing ground to Germany, Manchester was unable to find posts for its men as works chemists. The First World War swallowed up all available young graduates, but employment problems returned with its ending. The early months of 1919 were marked by a glut of ex-officers (as well as other ranks) looking for employment. There were, according to the London board, some 10,000 unplaced officers in London alone. The situation was helped, however, by the low numbers of men graduating from the universities, and possibly by the post-war Aliens Act. (This act required that a permit be obtained from the Ministry of Labour for each foreigner employed. His wages were not to be lower than the wages usually received by a British employee for similar work.) It was also helped by the 1919–20 economic boom, which encouraged firms to take on extra men. There were the beginnings of shortages in some skills when the sudden but deep depression descended. The next few years were very difficult for graduates looking for work. Graduates with the new commerce degree from the LSE needed all the help the School could give them to find a post. The London board made the point in its 1924–25 report that there was 'a dearth of posts for young Engineering and Chemistry Graduates', and more posts would have to be created for these, and other graduates, before really satisfactory employment conditions could arise. In 1925 the universities were still being warned by the government against overstocking the market for chemists.[27] ICI advised the public schools in 1927 that both the chemical and engineering professions were perhaps overcrowded. The industrial situation was much improved by 1928, but the demand from industry was still insufficient to absorb all the chemistry graduates, and this despite the heavy recruitment of chemists by the newly-formed Imperial Chemical Industries. During the good year of 1928–29, the manufacturing houses wanted an unusually high number of Cambridge men in the administrative and distribution sides of their businesses. In 1929, more Cambridge graduates found their way into manufacturing houses as trainees, on both the commercial and the technical sides of business.

The demand for graduates had risen with the rise in economic confidence in the late 1920s, but it fell with the economic downturn of 1930. A feature of the world depression in trade and industry in the late 1920s and early 1930s was the heavy unemployment which hit the clerical, administrative, and professional grades, as well as the front-line manual workers. Britain, partly for the reason that the depression affected it less forcibly than many other countries, and partly for the reason that the numbers of trained young people leaving British universities were proportionately fewer, was less troubled by the 'frustrated intellectual'. But job prospects were much curtailed, and 'under-employment' – in the sense of trained personnel accepting work well below their capacity – became widespread. Then graduates began losing their jobs. The heaviest unemployment was in the chemical, engineering, and allied industries. Demand began to pick up again by 1934, although still during 1935–36 the London board reported 'a considerable number' of chemists and biological scientists available for employment. London's engineers were more easily placed, although

the opportunities available are not, of course, all equally desirable – many men have been employed in work of a routine character, offering little immediate scope – but the rapid and continuing expansion of, for example, the aircraft industry, has provided immediate employment for a number of new Graduates, many of whom could not, in former years, have hoped for a post for some time.

Rearmament changed the picture for technical men, and for the first time demand ran high.

The trend of increasing demand for technical graduates continued through the Second World War and into the 1950s. But after the war this high demand only applied to the best of the graduates; demand for the 'average' man with science and engineering skills was much less strong. Arts graduates had a very hard time finding jobs after the Second World War, prompting the Chairman of the Cambridge board to write to the Chancellor of the Exchequer in 1948, 'expressing the Board's grave concern over the matter of providing suitable employment for the increased output of Arts graduates, resulting from the expansion which Universities are undertaking in accordance with Government policy ...'.[28] But, by the early 1950s, industrial demand had increased markedly. Demand grew, not for the 'average arts man' but primarily for men with 'leadership qualities', and also for good graduates with accountancy skills. The depression of 1958–59 was reflected in another sharp drop in graduate recruitment.

Industrial demand for female graduates had been almost non-existent. Most female graduates had expected to become teachers, but a small number had been willing to enter, or at least had been prepared to contemplate entering, a business firm. Some slight demand usually occurred towards the end of the periods of high demand for male graduates. Those who were recruited went primarily into secretarial or shop work; a few women scientists were able to avoid going into these 'female occupations'. There were always too many female graduates for the posts available. In 1924 the LSE commissioned an investigation into the openings for which female graduates might be suitable. The report painted a bleak picture. The 'testimony of Chambers of Commerce and Employment Bureaux shows fairly conclusively that in all parts of the country the supply of well-trained women is far in excess of the demand. It is only in the case of nurses, housekeepers and mothers'-helps that there is no difficulty in obtaining posts.'[29] Female graduates seem to have been equally unwanted by British industry whatever their university, and only 10 per cent were entering industry by the mid-1960s.

It might be argued that firms had wanted to recruit more young people from the higher education system, but the universities could not, or would not, supply them with men with the right skills; in short, that there was a skills gap in the supply from the higher education system. Certainly in some years more men with certain skills could have found work. The 'fit' between what was available and what firms demanded in any one year was not always close, particularly in years of economic buoyancy. There were, too, the justified complaints that much of the teaching in the universities did not bear industry very much in mind. It is also true that the products of a system which rested heavily upon an ability to pay the fees were not necessarily what industry was looking for. There were, however, no persistent gaps in the substantive skills leaving the universities over the first half of this century which left industry with an unmet demand. The evidence does not suggest that industry would normally have recruited more graduates in certain subjects had they been available, or that it would have recruited more graduates if they had been trained with more emphasis on an industrial career. Those whose job it was in the professional associations and universities to place young people found no unmet demand. Rather they saw that demand would have to be created. The Institute of Chemistry, whose members had both higher education and practical experience, recorded that in 1914 one-seventh of the members of the institute were abroad 'because of lack of home opportunity'.[30] A government committee set up in the mid-1920s, after extensive enquiries into the manpower needs of Britain's main manufacturing industries, found no evidence that a gap in supply existed. It concluded in 1929 that the facilities offered by the higher education system were 'more than equal to the effective demand from industry and trade'.[31] The supply of technically trained men was sufficient for the rapidly expanding industrial sectors, like electrical engineering – where there was a 'plentiful supply of well-trained and technically competent men to fill the executive and managerial posts' – and to the more sluggish sectors like shipbuilding, where the demand was 'more than met by the supply'.[32] A second committee looking at advanced courses in technical schools came to a similar conclusion. 'In fact,' noted the committee, 'we have had practically no evidence from employers that they are unable to secure the establishment of any classes which they think desirable.'[33] ICI noted in 1937 that 'the desire to find occupation in ICI brings forth an automatic stream of applications for appointment by well qualified men'.[34] The Advisory Council on Science Policy decided in 1947 that 'The primary reason why our industry as a whole does not make more use of scientists (including technologists) is not because their members were, and are, insufficient, but because large sections of industry, being conservative and complacent, have neither missed nor asked for them.'[35]

Education had attempted, at least in the early part of the century, to offer more of a vocational rather than an academic training to students considering a career in industry. The universities had been very susceptible to the idea of providing an educational service to industry, and they made strong moves to satisfy what they hoped were industry's requirements (see Chapter 5). The new universities, emerging from lower-level technical and arts colleges, were well used to meeting, or trying to meet, the needs of the local business community. Their continual financial difficulties helped to overcome much of the internal resistance to a close relationship with industry after they had achieved university status. The ancient universities, for their part, had become aware that the new universities being set up with such acclaim in many of the country's wealthiest towns were presenting them with a challenge, and that some moves towards the industrial world might be necessary. They feared that if they did not make some move towards an education more relevant to a business career, wealthy businessmen might begin sending their sons to the new universities.[36]

Even before the First World War, it had become clear that the efforts of the educationalists, encouraged by men of affairs and some businessmen, to begin to offer vocational as well as academic training in universities would not be reciprocated by British employers. Industry acknowledged no obligation to recruit the men being trained in the universities. Firms continued to recruit as and when they wanted a man, taking no account of the time-scale or numbers needed by the universities to keep the efforts going. Instead they made short-term and fluctuating demands. The graduates that education had hoped would be taken by industry were too often likely to remain unemployed, or at least under-employed. Educationalists' interest in providing a relevant education was not sustained. They saw little to be gained in attempting to prepare men for industry when industry showed so little want of them. By the 1930s the universities had become very wary of even gearing the numbers of graduates to industry's 'needs'. H. T. Tizard of Imperial College, in an address to the British Association in 1934, stated bluntly that

It is a far better policy deliberately to keep the supply somewhat short of the demand; the world will not appreciably suffer if any particular application of science to industry and agriculture develops rather more slowly than the enthusiast could wish, and there are few spectacles more distressing than that of the highly educated specialist who is unemployed through no fault of his own, and whose training and interests do not fit him for other work.

Forecasts of future shortages began to be greeted with a high degree of scepticism. Thus the numbers of qualified men being produced in certain specialisms were as far as possible kept deliberately in tune with the numbers thought likely to be absorbed by the labour market – and these numbers erred on the side of caution.

British employers did face great difficulties when they took on men from higher education, and these adversely affected demand. Many firms experimenting with graduates for possible future management found that they were not very good at choosing men who would be successful. But it was critical that they chose well if they had management in mind for them. The system of recruiting large numbers of clerks and choosing just a few for more responsible posts allowed a much wider margin of error in recruitment in comparison with the system of recruiting very small numbers of men as potential managers. Industrialists attributed this problem of not choosing well partly to their own lack of experience with this different type of recruit. The choices were usually made by only one member of the firm, often a top executive or the owner, and their personal idiosyncracies could end in mistakes which were both painful and costly. Too many mistakes prompted some firms to set up committees to conduct the interviews. Other selection procedures were tried in the post-1945 period when it was found that the success rate was still unacceptably low. One of the most progressive firms in the recruitment of graduates, Unilever, set up a panel of 100 selectors from its top managers, and submitted the applicants to various psychological tests, interviews, and discussions of business problems. The system underwent continual refinements, and 'in so far as experience, common sense and scientific method could be combined to reduce the risks of error, the selection process seemed to offer a fair and reasonable avenue of progress'.[37]

While some firms acknowledged their own lack of expertise in choosing men with potential from the universities, many more felt that their choice had been restricted. The fault for this was sometimes laid at the door of the university appointments boards. Firms thought they were not being offered the best men that the boards had available. More often, however, they complained that good men were not choosing industry as a career. Industry knew that there was never, except in wartime, a shortage of graduates for it to recruit, but it also knew that its image was generally a poor one and this was acting as a deterrent to men with a choice.

The image was partly deserved. There were many aspects of working in business which graduates found very unattractive. Employers, first of all, often did not know what to do with graduates when they got them. A common response was to ignore the fact that they were graduates. They set them on work which a non-graduate could do perfectly well, and then left them to make their own way out of it if they could. The general levels of pay were not attractive, at least until the late 1950s, and the salary an individual might rise to in a firm was always deliberately shrouded in mystery. There were high salaries to be had for the occasional man, but they were too few in number for that to affect industry's image as a low payer. Early in the century it was not unusual for new raw men, whether school-leaver or graduate, to be allowed little or no wage: they could not, unlike teachers, expect to be allowed to learn the job at the employer's expense. This applied equally to apprentices, whose training costs were covered either by the work of the apprentices or by a premium paid by their parents. A survey of graduates in 1910 noted that 'Many a man towards the end of his university career, discovers for the first time that he has nothing to offer in the industrial or commercial market in return for a salary.'[38] In Lloyds Bank before 1914 the few graduates who were recruited started at the bottom and received no pay for six months. John Lewis began in 1926 a scheme which required each recruit to earn a set sum each week for the firm before they were entitled to a wage. If they did not earn this set sum they became in debt to the firm for the deficient amount. Starting salaries could be very low for a man in his early twenties. Selfridges in the 1920s were offering 'keen young graduates' 5s a week with free lunches and teas. Most large engineering firms offered some form of pupillage course to new graduates by the

1930s ('with great benefit to themselves', according to ICI), but the men had to be able to live on a nominal wage for up to three years, and some could not. In railway engineering, graduates could be faced with a six months' probationary period without any pay. And whilst there was the possibility of good wages later in a man's career, there was often great uncertainty attached to future pay increases along the way, particularly in manufacturing industry. Young men 'are naturally put off', observed one Oxford don discussing the wages paid by industry in the 1930s, 'by people who offer them the prospect of years of hackwork at a starvation wage and expect them to be grateful'.[39]

There was, too, industry's deserved reputation for retaining poor quality managers and ancient directors; a double drawback for a young man who was ambitious. The reputation sat alongside another for easy and arbitrary dismissals of newer, unprotected men. This latter made industry seem a more risky occupation than, for example, the Civil Service. Graduates writing back to the appointments boards mentioned dismissals after only two days' employment, after one week, after three months, and at the end of a two-year training programme – often for unsuitability. Others were dismissed after many years for reasons of economy. ICI dismissed large numbers, possibly up to 1,000, of its young people in the difficult years of the early 1930s. Dismissal took on major importance in the inter-war period when good posts were hard to come by without influence. Add to this the unpleasant working environment of much of manufacturing industry, and industry was right to believe its image did not help to attract men who had a choice.

But added to the unfavourable image there was a high degree of prejudice which would have helped to deter graduates considering a career. The objectives of industry – as they were generally understood – and the means to achieve them, were held in very low regard. Manufacturers were thought to have as their main aim the accumulation of profits to the detriment of both the work-force and the environment. The 'cleaner' money-making in the City, far removed from productive industry and near to the centres of power, was much more acceptable. An occupation in shipping could also be admitted to in polite society. Most important, for some graduates, was the low social status of businessmen. Whilst leading industrial families could enjoy high prestige in provincial towns, a business career did not itself attract prestige. Any association with manual work automatically downgraded a position. Manual work, unless it was for recreation or on one's own farm, was associated with the lower classes and thus to be avoided. Engineers, in spite of their long and expensive training and their energy in forming themselves into professions, were not accorded high status – their connection with manufacturing helped to preclude their full acceptance in Britain as 'professional men'. Scientists, who worked at a greater distance from the shop-floor, clung to their superiority over engineers. Manufacturers themselves were not immune to this kind of thinking. A Cambridge survey in 1945 reported that scientists and engineers were regarded as being in a lower category than graduates without technical qualifications and employed in administration. It concluded that 'There is a fundamental snobbery running through our whole social system which tends to regard those who deal with organisation and finance as superior to those who deal with research and production.'[40] It could have added that those who entered a profession or the higher ranks of the Civil Service still attracted rather more status than the man in a business career of any kind.

Business was right to believe that its intake of men was not of the highest intellectual level. Just before the Second World War, for Cambridge males, the intellectual level of those entering business – where intellect was judged by the class of degree taken – was not so high as that of men entering certain other occupations. In 1937 the *number* of first-class honours men entering commerce and industry compared well with, for example, government service or teaching. But in the *proportion* of first-class honours men of those entering each occupation, industry and commerce compared most unfavourably. First-class honours men made up over half of those who entered academic research, one-quarter of those in government service, and some 16 per cent of those entering teaching – but only 14.8 per cent of those entering the scientific side of industry, and a mere 4.2 per cent of those entering commerce. Commerce, indeed, found itself in 1937 with an intake of Cambridge men 69 per cent of whom had less than a second-class honours degree.[41] The figures are somewhat worse for the following year. However, this was largely a consequence of industry's own choice. When firms went to the universities for men, their emphasis was on personality, not formal qualifications, and high

formal qualifications could deter them. Some of the largest manufacturing firms held the view that 'too much stress should not be
laid on ability to pass examinations. In general it is more important that candidates should have taken an active part in social and
athletic activities and be good mixers.'[42] Firms looking for potential managers in the mid-1950s still exhibited a strong preference
for personal qualities over academic qualifications, even for technical graduates.[43] A British Institute of Management study group
in 1955 stated without reservation that 'In all types of graduate
the decisive factor in management quality will be the innate quality
of the man himself, irrespective of the precise nature of his qualifications.'[44] Henry Mond of ICI seems to have been one of the few
businessmen who demanded both personality and high academic
ability in his new recruits. Complaining to the Cambridge University appointments board in 1929 about the men the board was
offering ICI at that time, Mond explained,

What is wanted is a man who takes First or Second Class Honours, who
plays Rugby Football or Cricket or any of the major sports, for his
University, who is president of the J.C.R. of his College, or in non-col-
legiate universities, is elected by his fellow undergraduates to the Students Representative Council, who is not afraid of 'losing his dignity'.[45]

When a firm did finally recruit a graduate he brought uncertainties and difficulties into the firm. There was, firstly, almost always
the resistance of the other employees to the innovation. Recruitment from the universities was sometimes seen as an implied
criticism of existing staff and their education, and a threat to their
prospects. Where the unions became involved with white-collar
workers they demanded equality of opportunity, and looked upon
university graduates with distaste, at least until after the widening
of educational opportunities after the Second World War. Graduates were not thought of as fair competition but as men who,
having already had the privilege of an expensive education, were
now exploiting that privilege at the school-leaver's expense. Insist-
ence on promotion by seniority seemed to be the only effective
safeguard against them. The lower levels of management thought
themselves particularly threatened. Even in the 1950s, the graduate
was still considered to be a man with unfair advantages both
inside the firm and in society, which had to be resisted. A survey
of nationalised industries in 1951 noted that

The persistent belief that management favours its own class in making promotions leads, not surprisingly, to the strongest objection to the entry of university graduates at a high point on the ladder and destined for senior posts. The objection is constantly made that they lack the practical experience to manage effectively, but beneath all this lies the feeling that they have come up by an easier route and enjoyed advantages – not only educational advantages – which the complainant missed.[46]

It was not unusual for graduates to hide the fact that they were graduates, even from their employers. Often class differences militated against the easy acceptance of graduates into firms with no tradition of such men coming in at the lower levels. At best, the differences produced misunderstandings: at worst, the snobbery on the part of some graduates and the prejudice on the part of some non-graduates produced relationships detrimental to the good management of the firm.

There was also the problem of placing the graduate in a department where he could be of some use after the usual small amount of on-the-job training. Scientists and engineers were most easily placed. What success there was in absorbing university graduates into British firms – and it was still limited and patchy in the 1950s – lay chiefly with the scientists and engineers. It was also possible for men with skills in accounting, economics, or actuarial work to fit into large functionally-departmentalised firms since such men could be catalogued with other men using similar skills. But arts graduates, with no apparent business skills, had to be found a home. Only the largest firms could absorb more than a handful in non-technical departments, in sales or personnel. The Morgan Crucible Company advised in 1938 that 'without specialist knowledge in engineering, science, or accountancy, it may be impossible to obtain a post presenting opportunities of advancement without influence'.[47] After the Second World War, when there was a shortage of good technical graduates, some firms took on arts graduates and gave them sufficient technical training to enable them to take on work in production.

Once a firm began to recruit graduates, management was faced with the problem of the level at which they should enter. Many placed the graduates at the lowest level. This allowed them to argue that graduates and school-leavers were being given equal treatment and the same opportunities for promotion. They did the same type of work and competed against each other for promotion when a vacancy occurred. There was a widespread dislike amongst industrialists of encouraging (or allowing) a 'crown prince' attitude to develop among the non-family graduates in their employ. They argued that managers who had to work their way up gained advantages: they understood what happened at the lower levels; a gap in understanding was less likely to develop between the management and the men; the firm enjoyed a continuity of personnel; and it provided a means of rewarding long-serving staff. 'Coming up the hard way' gave a chance of promotion to those without influence.

But entering at the lowest level in a British firm held few attractions for graduates. Many of them found the years in a junior capacity, along with the uncertainty which always surrounded promotion prospects, very irksome. 'One just has to go on getting older, which is not too easy if you know that the authorities fully intend to make you an officer in due course, but worse if there is any uncertainty about their intentions.'[48] Arts graduates in junior posts were more than likely, particularly in the early part of the century, to be involved in performing very routine and repetitive clerical tasks. Whilst machinery was available to deal with many of them, it was not rapidly adopted by British firms. Mechanisation was spreading amongst Britain's most forward-looking firms in the inter-war period, and the major banks were beginning to mechanise their bookkeeping systems by the late 1920s, but it was still not unusual to find firms as late as the 1950s continuing with systems more appropriate to the 1900s. In the National Mutual Assurance Society – a company under the chairmanship of J. M. Keynes for many years – a clerk 'would have found the policy registers still bound in half-calf, still being written-up by hand. He would have found himself, together with many others, working out each member's bonus by individual calculation and after all had been checked, writing the answers with pen and ink on notices to be sent to the members.'[49] Moreover, British firms mechanised without confidence and without taking full advantage of the possibilities. Mechanisation tended to be used merely to take over repetitive tasks previously done by hand, rather than to revolutionise existing work practices and thus open up new and rewarding positions for able staff. One insurance company commented that 'It is difficult to provide for a regular influx of University-trained men without establishing a kind of double grade in the service.' It also recognised, however, that 'If this course were successful in producing satisfactory candidates for the higher posts it would react unfavourably on the prospects of the boys coming straight from school, and the consequence of this might be very unfortunate.'[50] The idea of lateral promotion, or of 'bridges' between promotional ladders, was very slow to permeate through British industry.

The drop-out rate of graduates was high enough to give businessmen pause for thought. The publishers William Heinemann were only one firm which found that quite a number of recruits faded out during the first eighteen months. The Edinburgh University appointments board suggested that commerce graduates had a better record of staying in industry than arts graduates, and that was because whilst the arts graduate 'finds a difficulty in adapting himself to the accurate detail of a junior post, and to business conditions in general, with the result that he has frequently left business for another career after a comparatively short period', the commerce graduate's university training had prepared him rather better, both technically and psychologically, for the transfer into industry.[51] Where the graduate stayed on, the firm ran the risk that after years of routine work the man would become less able to take responsibility. The early years in insurance companies, according to one graduate employed by the Sun Insurance Office, 'stultifies so many of them'.[52]

All the difficulties, however, were demonstrably capable of being overcome to a large extent. British business had the example of a number of firms which were able to solve one or more of them. Employers who were determined to have good graduates had little difficulty attracting them. Barr and Stroud (manufacturers of highly specialised mechanical, electrical and optical gear for the armed forces, with around 3,000 employees) could report in 1939 that 'All Directors hold University Honours Degrees. The majority of the staff are University Graduates.'[53] Thomas Hedley (a subsidiary of the US corporation Proctor and Gamble) counted in its Manufacturing Division in 1938 sixty-nine graduates out of the ninety-one people holding responsible positions. Neither was it necessary to pay very high salaries to attract them – ICI's rates in some divisions were far from generous. Companies with a will got their best and brightest recruits into top posts before they ossified. In ICI's Alkali Group in the late 1930s young managers were confident that their abilities would be recognised with promotion. In its Fertilisers Group there were directors on the Group board in their early thirties. British businessmen were not unwilling to admit that they rejected university men not simply because of the difficulties of recruiting and absorbing graduates, large though these difficulties were, but because of their low level of interest in the men that higher education produced.

Businessmen and graduates have recorded the fact that higher education was seen quite widely as being a positive disadvantage to a business career. The 'typical' graduate was seen as very inappropriate material for British firms. He was, when he left his university, too old. The early years in industry were thought to be critical for forming the right habits and ideas. This was particularly so in banking, where the dull routine work 'was of assistance in forming steadiness of character and habits of industry and patience, without which a successful career in a Bank is impossible'.[54] The 'typical' graduate had, moreover, been spoiled in industry's eyes for a business career. University life – the long holidays, the freedom to make choices, the importance given to a pleasant sports and social life – unsettled young men for business. 'Sometimes when a man has been through a long course of philosophy and higher thinking, it was difficult to get him to learn shorthand or attend to some routine that did not appeal to him.'[55] This criticism did not apply only to men graduating from Oxbridge. 'Unfortunately,' wrote one employer in 1955 of a recently-resigned graduate, 'he had taken a degree in "Political Philosophy and Economics" at Glasgow University before joining us ... . These men are of little use and that is the common experience of all the British overseas banks. University life fits them for a more sheltered existence than we can offer.'[56] The suspicion in industry was that the university graduate was impatient with routine and with discipline, and looked for early promotion. He saw himself as an asset to be cultivated for positions of responsibility. Businessmen for their part saw no such asset. They saw a young man with a tendency to snobbishness, with too much theoretical knowledge and too little knowledge of industry, and the disadvantage of having spent his most pliable years outside the firm.

Unlike foreign employers, the British continued to see the 'typical' university graduate in terms of the arts graduate, and the arts graduate compared badly with the schoolboy recruit. The young boys who had entered the firm straight from school had gained three, four, or five years' experience before their early twenties: the new arts graduate had no experience. The schoolboy recruit had spent those years working hard: it was not doubted that the graduate had spent his time pleasantly and unprofitably. Yet he often expected a similar salary to his experienced counterpart. Lord Trent's reported view in 1950 was that 'The graduate going into industry will do well at the beginning of his career to forget that he has ever been to a university, and remember that for a while at any rate the messenger-boy knows more about the job than he does.'[57] Businessmen generally could see little in the university arts man to offset such major defects: 'B.A.' had little or no prestige. At best the arts graduate was a luxury good which could be taken up or put down according to the prosperity of the firm.

Higher education and British industry looked very much closer in the 1950s than they had done in the 1890s. From the early 1940s donations from industry to universities for industry-related subjects became less rare. More institutions were being used by companies for training. The new College of Aeronautical Science at Cranfield got off to a good start because the industry sent its men to be trained there. The firms nominated their men (usually older men) to Cranfield, paid their fees and accommodation charges, and could expect them to return at the end of their two-year training. The college relied on students from just one industry, but this industry – at least over Cranfield's first ten years – was in good shape and had no difficulty in attracting good science graduates. Another new post-war venture, the (privately funded) Administrative Staff College at Henley which offered short courses in management, also did well. Between 1946 and 1958 nearly 2,000 men (from business and the public services) passed through its doors – no mean achievement in British terms. In the 1950s university graduates, at least those of the 'right type', were being fêted and courted by large firms, and the annual recruiting 'milk round' began. The number of graduates being recruited into British business was rising markedly.

The change of attitude towards the graduate was, however, neither widespread nor radical. Many of the firms which were now recruiting graduates had turned to them reluctantly, and in the case of some firms, 'in desperation'. Their normal source of recruitment – bright young school-leavers from the grammar and public schools – was proving to be less fertile. Industrialists had begun to believe as early as the 1930s that higher education was attracting more of the most able young people who would normally have been available to them. Only about 5 per cent of secondary-school children went on to the universities and university teacher training departments by the onset of the Second World War, but the numbers of administrative, technical and clerical posts were opening up quite significantly in the 1930s, and firms were continually being warned that they would have to consider taking on men from the universities. In the post-1945 period, the belief was that the 'creaming-off' was increasing apace. Certainly the market for able school-leavers tightened. Employers of clerical labour, including the insurance companies, shipping companies, merchant houses, and banks became concerned over the future availability of good recruits. 'Even the accountancy firms, which had relied upon a plentiful supply of school leavers in the inter-war period, were alarmed that the increased facilities for sixth-form and university education would undermine the system of training under articles.'[58] Firms had to start looking at university men. In the clearing banks, although graduates were no longer passed over for recruitment, they in no way displaced the school-leaver as the preferred new entrant. As the chairman of Lloyds Bank explained in 1950, staff departments would be forced to recruit more entrants from the universities if they were to maintain the same type and standard of staff which they had come to expect before the Second World War: 'from this aspect, it would be the quality that we were after, not the university education *per se*'.[59] The universities were simply a source of able men which had to be tapped to get the numbers needed. It had also in the 1950s become fashionable to employ graduates.

The British government had at various times from the 1890s attempted to put pressure on businessmen to make better use of, and give more support to, the higher education system. Parliament itself had not given the subject of university education time for debate until 1954, but government committees and commissions had reported intermittently on the wide gap between British industry and education. A common response from industrialists was that education did not, and would not, produce what industry needed: education produced what it liked to produce and industry had to take it or leave it. The committees were not on the whole sympathetic to this line of argument. They agreed that education could, and should, be more alive to the needs of industry, but concluded that unless employers made it very clear what its needs were, and were prepared to back what they said with some action, education could not be expected to produce what was needed. But no common viewpoint of wants and needs could be discerned amongst industrialists. There were, for example, those employers who said and/or demonstrated that they were in favour of graduates. There were those against. There were those (the majority) who seem to have given the matter no thought. But those in favour, or against, were rarely in favour, or against, all types of graduates equally. Some were in favour of arts graduates and against business graduates. Some were in favour of engineering graduates, others totally opposed. There was little agreement on the role education should play in preparing graduates for their career and what should be left to the firm. The largest firms became increasingly interested in the 'personality' of the young graduate, some being quite prepared to ignore his academic qualifications. 'Average' men, they argued, were easily obtainable in all subjects. The Federation of British Industries (later the CBI) was used by governments as a general sounding-board of business opinion, but the Federation was never very decisive. It was always aware that its membership contained groups having very different preferences; and the size of the firm, its products or services, its technology, the quality of its directors, all worked together to produce different wants and needs. Education was left with the suspicion that industry would have insufficient interest in whatever it produced.

The various committees over the decades had also come face to face with the phenomenon of the difference between what industrialists *said* they wanted, and what they demonstrated they wanted by their actions. One committee in 1949 commented: 'Business leaders have told us that they value in their employees qualities which university education can foster. But these opinions hardly seem to find reflection in practice.'[60] Professor Zuckerman, in the 1960s, was more direct: 'we discovered in our successive inquiries that one of the least reliable ways for finding out what industry needs is to go and ask industry'.[61] A committee in 1979 reported on a very unhelpful phenomenon:

There is a conflict between the explicit statements made by employers and the implicit signals in the way that they select and recruit employees ... . Employers will give preference to the qualification which attracts the ablest candidates even if they would have preferred them to study something else. This then is fed back, perversely, to students as a message that the most popular course is the one best rewarded. The best students continue to choose that course and an enormous bias is created toward preserving the status quo.[62]

Education, or some parts of it, had made many attempts over the decades to respond specifically to what it thought were industry's wants and needs, either because industry had complained of a particular gap or because education had seen, or thought that it had seen, that a particular gap existed. Education usually had its fingers burned for its efforts. One of its most thankless efforts was the initiatives to provide a vocational education at university level for future businessmen.

References

1 (Robbins) Report, *Higher Education*, Cmnd. 2154, HMSO, 1963, p. 16.

2 Federation of British Industries (FBI), 'Memorandum on education by FBI Education Committee', January 1918, PRO ref. ED24/657.

3 E. W. Evans and N. C. Wiseman, 'Education, training and economic performance: British economists' views 1868–1939', *Journal of European Economic History*, Spring 1984, p. 138.

4 (Malcolm) Report, *Education and Industry (England and Wales)*, Part 1, HMSO, 1927; Part 2, HMSO, 1928, p. 28.

5 M. Sanderson, *Educational Opportunity and Social Change in England*, Faber and Faber, 1987, p. 26.

6 FBI, 'Report of education committee on compulsory continued education under the Education Act of 1918', July 1919, P. R. O. ref. ED24/657.

7 Political and Economic Planning (PEP), *The Entrance to Industry*, PEP, 1935, p. 48.

8 R. W. Ferguson, ed., *Training in Industry*, Pitman, 1935, p. 12.

9 FBI, Annual Report, 1925, p. 9. Warwick ref. MSS 200/F/4/2/8–14.

10 (Malcolm) Report, Part 2, p. 24.

11 FBI report, January 1918, p. 4.

12 FBI, *Bulletin*, 12 April 1920, p. 226.

13 S. Cotgrove, *Technical Education and Social Change*, George Allen and Unwin, 1958, p. 65.

14 *Nature*, 15 September 1910, p. 349.

15 Manchester Chamber of Commerce, *Monthly Record*, 29 April 1905, p. 87.

16 L. Urwick and E. F. L. Brech, *The Making of Scientific Management: Management in British Industry*, II, Management Publications Trust, 1946, p. 114.

17 P. L. Robertson, 'Technical education in the British shipbuilding and marine engineering industries, 1863–1914', *Economic History Review*, May 1974, p. 233.

18 (Lord) Eustace Percy, *Education at the Crossroads*, Evans Bros., 1930, p. 66.

19 PEP, *The Entrance to Industry*, p. 15.

20 *The Times*, 16 April 1943, 5c.

21 G. L. Payne, *Britain's Scientific and Technological Manpower*, Stanford University Press, Stanford, CA, 1960, p. 234.

22 P. F. R. Venables, *Technical Education: Its Aims, Organisation and Future Development*, G. Bell and Sons, 1956 ed., p. 199.

23 University of Manchester, Report of the Council to the Court of Governors, 13 November 1908, p. 17, ref. UA/23.

24 (Spens) Report, *University Education and Business*, Cambridge University Press, 1945, p. 18.

25 Political and Economic Planning, 'Graduates' jobs', *Planning*, XXI, 24 October 1955, pp. 193–207.

26 The records of those consulted are listed on pp.00–00.

27 University of Birmingham, Report of the Principal to the Council, 1924–25, p. 11.

28 University of Cambridge Appointments Board (UCAB), annual report 1948.

29 E. A. H. Pearson, 'Openings for University Women', unpublished report, 1924, p. 28, available in the British Library of Political and Economic Science (BLPES).

30 R. B. Pilcher, *History of the Institute: 1877–1914*, The Institute of Chemistry, p. 45.

31 (Balfour) Committee, *Industry and Trade*, Final Report, HMSO, 1929, Cmd. 3282, p. 212.

32 (Balfour) Committee, *Industry and Trade: Factors in Commercial and Industrial Efficiency*, HMSO, 1927, pp. 195–6.

33 (Malcolm) Report, Part 2, p. 40.

34 ICI, Memorandum, 'The training of personnel', September 1937, file: Staff recruitment and training, Box 274.

35 A. Guagnini, 'Technical education in late-nineteenth century Britain: the case of Manchester', unpublished paper for LSE conference, 9 September 1988, p. 2.

36 *Cambridge University Reporter*, 14 May 1903, p. 774.

37 C. Wilson, *Unilever 1945–1965*, Cassell, 1968, p. 50.

38 *Nature*, 15 September 1910, p. 345.

39 UCAB, undated memorandum, ref. APTB 14/12 (1–9).

40 Spens, *University Education*, p. 14.

41 Spens, *University Education*, p. 64.

42 Management Research Group One, 'Report on selection, training and development of executives', March 1938, ref. 723.

43 PEP, *Graduates in Industry*, George Allen and Unwin, 1957, p. 16.

44 British Institute of Management, *Recruitment and Training of Men Intended for Management Positions*, BIM, 1955, p. 15.

45 ICI, note from H. Mond, 22 July 1927, file CR/215/7, box 457.

46 Acton Society Trust, *Problems of Promotion Policy*, Nationalised Industry Pamphlet, 1951, p. 6.

47 UCAB, Firms' Replies, 28 November 1938, ref. APTB 14/13 (72–89).

48 UCAB, Graduates' Replies, 19 March 1939, ref. APTB 14/14.

49 E. Street, *The History of the National Mutual Life Assurance Society, 1830–1980*, National Mutual Life Assurance Society, 1980, p. 55.

50 UCAB, Firms' Replies, 31 October 1938, ref. APTB 14/13 (72–89).

51 H. Rostron, *Report on Education for Higher Positions in Commerce*, The Association for Education in Industry and Commerce, 1929, p. 40.

52 UCAB, Graduates' Replies, 19 May 1939, ref. APTB 14/14.

53 UCAB, 2 May 1939, ref. APTB 14/12 (1–9).

54 Ministry of Labour, Choice of Careers Series Booklet, *Banking*, HMSO, 1939, p. 11.

55 *The Times*, 29 April 1930.

56 I am grateful to Dr G. Jones for this reference from the archives of the British Bank of the Middle East. Memorandum by General Manager for Board, 12 July 1955.

57 Management Research Groups Bulletin, 25 July 1950.

58 E. Green, *Debtors to their Profession: A History of the Institute of Bankers 1879–1979*, Methuen, 1979, p. 146.

59 Green, *Debtors*, p. 147.

60 (Carr-Saunders) Report, *Education for Commerce*, Ministry of Education, HMSO, 1949, p. 39.

61 In J. Mace, 'The shortage of engineers', *Higher Education Review*, X, Autumn 1977, p. 23.

62 Fifth Report from the Education, Science and Arts Committee, 1979–80, *The Funding and Organisation of Courses in Higher Education*, I, HMSO, 1980, p. 76.

Chapter 5

Attempts at management education

In 1989 the historian of the London Business School was expressing a commonly held view when he wrote that, 'apart from the Bachelor of Commerce degree offered at the London School of Economics from 1920 and at the universities of Birmingham and Edinburgh, the idea of scholarly training for business lay dormant from the time of Malachy Postlethwayte's proposal in the mideighteenth century until the first business schools in Britain were launched in 1964'.[1] This chapter will show that the idea of scholarly training for business had been much more alive than is usually suggested. But it will also show that the practical expressions of this idea were all rejected by business, and they remained small and underdeveloped.

Supporters of the idea of a relevant, university-level education for aspiring managers launched strong initiatives in three periods before the Second World War. These were in the late 1890s, just after the First World War, and in the late 1920s. The three periods had seemed very propitious for this type of initiative. The main reason for the optimism was that in each period the economy was buoyant, and when the economy was buoyant higher education could expect to benefit. From a buoyant economy flowed, firstly, an increased industrial demand for university graduates, which, although always low, was much affected by business conditions. The higher business demand for graduates, in turn, affected student demand for university training. Secondly, a buoyant economy gave rise to hopes of rather more generous donations from industry. This was particularly the case just after the First World War when not only was there an economic boom, but also the knowledge that many businesses had done very well out of the war.

There was some sensitivity in the business world to the charges of profiteering, and educationalists hoped that this would help loosen purse-strings. Hopes were raised when the British oil companies proposed to hand over the enormous sum of £210,000 for a Chemical School at Cambridge.[2] A leading oilman, Robert Waley Cohen, was a Cambridge graduate and an active supporter of the University, but the move was none the less encouraging. As well as the helpful state of business confidence, there was also in these three periods the knowledge that the number of potential students which might be attracted to the courses was agreeably large. In the late nineteenth century, when son or nephew would normally expect to take over from the present head of the firm, the potential market of business heirs was a sizeable one. This was joined by the growing numbers of young men able to afford a (civic) university education for a career in business. Business itself by the end of the century was becoming less unacceptable as an occupation for the sons of the middle classes: they had to be placed somewhere. The public school population was expanding, and more of its members were needing assistance to find paid employment. The professionalisation of many business occupations, which raised their status, also helped to break down the middle-class parent's distaste. In the period immediately after the First World War, the numbers who might be interested in high-level courses for a business career surged because of the backlog of young people anxious to enter the universities. Many of these wanted an education relevant to a career, and business was a wide field. The *Manchester Guardian* reported in 1919 that industry was becoming more attractive as a career than the Civil Service. At the time of the third period, the late 1920s, it was known that some very large firms were turning to the universities for able men as potential managers. It seemed likely that large firms would now be interested in a business training for their future top men.

The initiatives were not undertaken for totally philanthropic reasons. The educationalists who most strongly supported them were primarily economists, who saw in a relevant education for managers opportunities for the development of their own subject. Economics as a discipline had branched out on its own only in the late nineteenth century and some economists, particularly those who were taking up posts in the new provincial colleges, were very amenable to providing courses which would attract larger numbers of students, and money for research. Many economists had turned their attention away from the concerns of orthodox political economy towards a more applied, or 'realistic', approach, based on empirical study. They were interested in all types of projects for economic and social reform. They shared the view that 'Economics should occupy a more prominent place than it has hitherto taken in the education of those intending to pursue a business life, and that the position assigned to it in English universities has heretofore been unreasonably confined.'[3] 'We are convinced', wrote the *Economic Journal* in 1902, 'that a rare opportunity is at the present moment offered to Economics, and that it may gain a position of great influence, if it can succeed in demonstrating that it is *the* "science of business".'[4] The new university colleges, for their part, supported the idea of what was at first called 'higher commercial education'. They had begun to aim for full university status at the turn of the century and for this they needed quite substantial sums of money. Their appeals to industry for financial help stressed the relevance to business of the training they gave, and the idea of an education specifically designed for future managers seemed to offer them further ammunition for their cause.

Britain was some years behind a number of other countries in offering a business education at university level. France already had its prestigious Écoles des Hautes Études Commerciales, Belgium its Institut Supérieur de Commerce at Antwerp, Germany its Handelshochschulen, Japan its well-known Tokyo Higher Commercial School, and the US the Wharton School of Finance and Economy. But Britain's late start did mean that it could learn from others' experiences, as *they* had learned from Britain in so many areas earlier in the century. British economists went abroad to look, and they emphasised in their reports to British businessmen that the UK's competitors were already benefiting from their investment in the young people who would in the future be managing their large firms. The economists offered to provide a similar educational service to British firms.

What they had in mind to offer depended to some extent on the type of business carried on in the environs of each university. The civics were self-consciously regional rather than, like Oxford and Cambridge, national institutions. Thus London stressed the needs of the financial services sector, Birmingham the metal trades, Manchester the cotton industry. They also had to bear in mind the type of recruit likely to be attracted to the training – Birmingham saw its market as businessmen's heirs, London would attract ambitious clerks. But all the initiatives offered a three-layered approach. It began with an introduction to the world of industry and individual industries. This was followed by training in specific skills, like statistics, accounting, and languages. The final stage covered an introduction to the various divisions, or functions, of business (buying, selling, production, finance, transport, industrial relations) and their co-ordination in the firm. This was all to be interspersed with bouts of work experience. Birmingham, whose hopes lay in attracting the sons of industrialists, stressed policy-making rather more.

The proponents of the new higher commercial education had to walk a tightrope between attracting business interest to a practical yet wide training, and finding acceptance for the subject as one suitably 'liberal' for a university to offer. To its supporters a liberal education was concerned with the transmission of culture, the development of intellect, and the moulding of personality. What it was not was the transmission of knowledge directly relevant to trade and manufacturing industry. As in Japan, Germany, and the US in the nineteenth century, traditional education-alists looked on this new type of education, with its emphasis on relevance and practicality, as a threat rather than an opportunity, and more suitable to a technical college which trained for low-level occupations than a university which trained for life. British reformers argued that 'liberal' could be applied to modern as well as to ancient subjects, and that they intended in any case to offer to industry what the universities had offered in previous centuries and what they were now offering to some extent to medicine, the Church, and the law. Education for these high-level occupations, or professions, was both liberal and relevant. Sir William Beveridge noted in 1921 that 'Even the Oxford "Greats" course had its mundane uses, as a direct training for the more solemn forms of journalism, and as a passport to the Higher Civil Service.'[5]

The analogy of business training with medical training became a popular one in an effort to emphasise that the men would experience both theory and practice. Medical students spent much of their time in the hospital as, it was hoped, business students would spend much of their time in the firm. The analogy was also used to try and counter industry's argument that many unsuitable men would be trained, since potential managers could only be identified by performance on-the-job. The business student would be in no worse a position than the medical student: the risk of unsuitability was no greater. There was, too, the query as to how the universities could teach something for which they themselves had had no proper training. The response was that UK education-alists were in a comparable position to those in other countries. These were taking up the challenge by tapping expertise from many sources and building up a corpus of knowledge through research. Foreign institutions, moreover, especially in Japan, had recruited a number of excellent teachers from Britain and kept them until their own people were ready to take over. Many of the early teachers in the British university faculties of commerce had had direct experience of business, and they could employ practising businessmen – bankers, railwaymen, accountants, engineers – to lecture on their own industries and specialisms.

The stance of conservative academics was thrown somewhat off-centre when it was pointed out that their own universities could not afford to ignore an idea which might attract badly needed students and funds. The older universities found the discussions on higher commercial education painful, and eventually neither totally rejected the idea nor fully accepted it. In allowing some development in economics (a degree at Cambridge, a diploma at Oxford), they hoped that this might also satisfy those interested in a relevant education for those destined for a business career. The University of London also allowed a degree in economics, at the London School of Economics.

The new universities in Britain at this time were in a similar position to the new institutions abroad, since they all expected to enjoy a closer relationship with industry outside the old university system. Whether the British civic universities could succeed, as the German *Hochschulen* had succeeded, in becoming a different but equal set of institutions to the old universities, depended to a large extent on the level of support they received from industry. The foreign initiatives survived and prospered because the demand for what they produced had been a strong one.

The new London School of Economics was amongst the first to want to offer a business degree, in 1901. The School had been set up in 1895 on the initiative of Sidney Webb, using a small bequest and other small sums collected from a number of sources which Webb and his associates were able to tap. The purposes of the School were, unusually in the British context, grounded in both research and teaching. They were 'the fundamental study of society and its institutions' and 'teaching of a practical commercial value'.[6] Student numbers for both the day and evening courses had been satisfactory from its inception, and when the School became part of the University of London in 1901, it applied to offer a degree in commerce. The attempt to establish a Faculty of Commerce failed because the University of London commissioners would not agree to it, but they did allow a Faculty in Economics and Political Science (including Commerce and Industry), and the School set up its B.Sc. (Econ.).

Unfortunately for everybody, economics – even the 'realistic' economics which was being developed in the new universities – was not an attractive thought outside a small circle of academics, and the title of the new degree was not one to excite business interest. While the foundations of the economics degree were being laid down, the School continued with its stated intention of serving the educational needs of young people in business. From its beginnings in 1895 its well-qualified teachers had offered statistics, economics, railway economics, commercial law, banking and finance. It was able to continue after 1901 to offer courses at below degree level to men and women working in the capital's commercial and financial houses. It also arranged directly with businesses for their training needs. In 1904, as a joint venture with the railway companies, it set up a Railway Department specifically to train railway employees in a wide range of subjects relevant to the administration of railway companies. A number of top managers from the railway companies formed themselves into a committee with the academics, to oversee the work. The companies paid the students' fees and seconded men to help with the teaching. They, most importantly, accorded status to the work being done. Lord Winterstoke, for example, chairman of the GWR, established in 1909 a silver medal to be awarded to distinguished students in the classes on railway administration.[7] In 1909, too, the students formed a Railway Students' Association which appears to have been very successful. Later, the Department moved into more advanced education work and the companies funded a Railway Research Service at the School. Apart from occasional differences of opinion between the School and the companies, the joint venture worked well, and only ended when the School found itself stretched to the limits of its resources after the Second World War. The School began a similar scheme with the insurance companies, but after two years the insurance companies transferred their interest to the newly-formed Institute of Insurance. The School's economics degree incorporated some subjects pertinent to a business career, most importantly accountancy (which the ancient universities had considered offering but had then rejected). There was no shortage of degree and other students (most of whom were part-time) for what was on offer. But the judgement long before the First World War was that all the efforts to arouse a wider business interest in the LSE's work had not had much success. London firms did not consider that the part-time courses attended by their staff were their concern; neither were they interested in recruiting young people with an economics degree, whatever its content. It has been judged that the LSE 'had emerged as a leading centre for a whole range of commercial subjects centred on economics and highly orientated towards inductive needs. As such it served as an exemplar to other universities in the 1900s.'[8]

The new universities at Birmingham and Manchester had been allowed to aim much more directly at an appropriate training for those intending a career in business management. These towns were major manufacturing and trading centres, and there was some optimism here that a tailor-made degree would indeed attract the required business support.

Birmingham: the Faculty of Commerce

The dominant force behind the new initiative of a Bachelor of Commerce degree at Birmingham was the same as that behind the proposed new university there – the energetic businessman and politician Joseph Chamberlain. The Chamber of Commerce had introduced the idea to him and he had taken it up with enthusiasm, basically as one more carrot to dangle before the businessmen of Birmingham whose money he wanted for the new university. Chamberlain pressed home to the industrialists of the Midlands the desirability of, and the necessity for, high-level vocational training for business, and the ability of the new university to provide it. 'In fact', he wrote, it is our aim to do for those engaged in commerce and manufacture what is now done for the professions of law and medicine, and while giving the general education which is calculated to train the mind and broaden the sympathies, we hope also to direct the instruction so as to be of practical advantage to those concerned.[9]

The Midlands industrialists were not persuaded sufficiently to give the idea their financial backing, but Chamberlain was able to turn to a non-industrial source for the necessary initial funds. He persuaded Lord Strathcona (the Canadian High Commissioner and sometime lecturer at Mason College) to allow his donation of £50,000 intended for the proposed University of Birmingham to be invested separately and the income used to support the new Faculty of Commerce.[10] It began in 1902 in two rooms over a shop.

The education that was offered to aspiring managers by the University of Birmingham was largely the creation of W. J. Ashley, an economist and the faculty's first Professor of Commerce. He visited Germany to look at the *Handelshochschulen*, and he copied ideas from both American and German universities. He intended the education 'not of the rank and file, but of the officers of the industrial and commercial army; those who, as principals, directors, managers, secretaries, heads of departments, etc. will ultimately guide the business activity of the country'.[11] The faculty would gear its teaching towards manufacturing industry, especially the ironworks of the Midlands. Birmingham, formerly unrivalled as the metal-goods centre of the world, was known to be losing out to foreign, particularly German, competition. Ashley had seen that the very successful Cologne Handelshochschule was well supported by the big manufacturing companies, which wanted 'men of all-round knowledge and business judgement'.[12] The B.Com. students in Birmingham would experience a broad, but relevant, full-time education based on established academic disciplines over the first two years, leading to a more specialised and vocational final year. They were to be offered some knowledge of a number of subjects considered relevant to a student expecting to reach top management in a manufacturing firm. These were economics, accounting, commercial law, public finance, sciences, and languages. They had also to take others, of their own choice, which came under the general heading 'cultural'. This was so flexible in practice that a commerce degree student could, and did, include a workshop course in engineering. There was, in addition, the weekly commerce seminar, 'the purpose of which is to train men in the investigation of commercial and economic questions, and to practice them in the presentation of their conclusions in a lucid way'. The final year was dominated by Commerce III, later called Business Policy,

in which we endeavour to put ourselves in the position of a business firm, and consider the various questions of policy which are likely to arise in the course of business proceedings, dealing with the organisation of a company, the financial arrangements, the laying out of the works, the whole question of policy with regard to prices, the means of disposing of goods, agencies, branches, and so forth, the question of advertising; and then very considerable attention is given to labour questions, and the various questions of shop discipline and wages, methods of remuneration, and so forth.[13]

The programme was intended to be sufficiently challenging to produce a trained mind; sufficiently stimulating to produce an educated mind; and sufficiently vocational to produce a mind ready to accept responsibility in the firm. Ashley had attracted good quality staff; they had business experience as well as high academic qualifications. But the whole initiative needed the participation of Birmingham industrialists to succeed. It needed industrial funding; it needed industrialists to send their sons for the training, and it needed opportunities to study business in operation.

The level of industry's interest in the new Faculty of Commerce was disappointing. However much thought and effort had gone into the business degree, Birmingham businessmen were never attracted to the idea. Ashley's first annual report recorded, realistically, that

our progress has been encouraging *under English circumstances*. When one considers the academic situation in England, the remarkable conservatism and inaccessibility to ideas displayed by that great central Middle Class which has hitherto sent its sons to no institution at all of higher training, one cannot but be pleased that it has proved possible to gather even a small class of regular students ... . The friends of the University must constantly bear in mind that the high-sounding designation 'Faculty of Commerce' is a Prophecy and an Ideal, rather than an accomplished Fact.

But the wealthy industrialists did not, either then or later, send their sons in sufficient numbers to be trained. Birmingham trades, with certain outstanding exceptions, were still predominately in private hands before the First World War and the leading industrial families, including the Chamberlains, were not prepared to send a son to Ashley. Without their example, other Midlands families would not consider sending their sons. The managing director of W. and T. Avery, who tried to help, confirmed to Ashley that 'Until it is a source of supply to the chief business houses of Birmingham parents will not send their sons to receive the advantages of the admirable training.'[14] Neither were Birmingham firms much interested in the men being produced. It had been expected initially that most of the graduates would have a post waiting for them, particularly as men without this advantage were not encouraged to apply. Only very able men without a job to go to were accepted and these were helped into local firms, usually in the position of assistant to a manager, by Ashley and his staff. But even these few were placed with great difficulty. The degree was accorded no value, and the graduates were older than Birmingham firms liked in new recruits.

Without the expectation of its leading to a career, the full-time commerce degree could attract only small numbers of men, and a high proportion of these were from abroad in the years before the First World War. Until 1919 the number of regular students in the department remained at under fifty, and only sixty-nine students in total had graduated. After 1919 there was a great influx of students, a phenomenon all universities experienced at this time, but by the mid-1920s the number of regular students in the faculty had again dropped back to under fifty. The 1930s saw no increase over the 1920s in the numbers of commerce graduates being produced. There were 156 in the 1930s, and 153 in the previous decade.[15]

Some general support from business, in the form of an Advisory Board, had begun in 1906, and over the next thirty years most local industrialists of note saw service on the board. But it seems not to have materially affected the fortunes of the degree. A later dean recorded that 'In my time, I never met a businessman in Birmingham with any useful ideas for the Faculty.'[16] The wider business community provided almost no direct financial support. Between 1901 and 1939 there was recorded only one contribution of any size – £5,000 in 1921 from the Mitsui Group of Japan to enable the Assistant Professorship of Commerce to be converted into a full-time Professorship of Finance.[17] In 1953 there was a donation of £7,000 for a lectureship. There was almost no money from business-funded research. An exception was Cadbury Brothers' funding, in 1925, of an industrial history of Birmingham. The university itself was not in a position to help with funds: its own position was very difficult right through until the 1930s.

The falling numbers of students enrolling for the B.Com. in the early 1920s, combined with the continuing lack of business interest and difficult employment situation, prompted some change of direction in 1925 when Ashley retired. The Principal expressed disappointment at the lack of support from those 'who have not yet realised what we can do for their sons and daughters',[18] and suggested that the faculty should broaden its objectives to include the training of others, such as economists and public administrators. Many other schemes were tried: in 1928 there was a new four-year B.Com. for science/commerce graduates (two years' science, two years' commerce); in 1932 there was set up a Joint Mining and Commerce Degree course. In 1944 the Faculty changed its name to the Faculty of Commerce and Social Science to reflect the growing importance of the social sciences at this time. After the Second World War it shared in the general expansion of student numbers and rising industrial demand for men with accountancy skills, and the faculty made new attempts to offer a business training at both undergraduate and graduate levels. Its first professor had been determined to provide Birmingham firms with a supply of men ready to take on responsibility and, with experience, prove their worth in the ranks of management. But the 'remarkable conservatism and inaccessibility to ideas' which Ashley had recognised in the 'great central Middle Class' of the 1900s had kept university education for managers an ideal in Birmingham rather than an accomplished fact for the next fifty years.

Manchester: the Faculty of Commerce and Administration

In 1904 Manchester, with the approval of the Manchester Chamber of Commerce, followed the example of Birmingham and instituted a degree designed to prepare young people for a career in business management. Commercial education had been offered for some time at below degree level, and Manchester had a large programme of lectures for the railway companies, and for people preparing for professional examinations. They also ran classes in, among other things, Chinese, to help the mercantile community make a better impact on that particular market, which 'given peace internal and external' was thought to be a promising one for the future.[19]

There was an initial disappointing response to appeals for financial support for the proposed B.Com. degree, but a public appeal eventually brought in almost £8,000. A calico printer provided an endowment of £10,000 for two-year scholarships. One year of this had to be spent abroad studying foreign business methods and then reporting on them for the benefit of British firms. The minimum amount of £1,500 a year for ten years which had been thought essential to launch the degree was not quite reached, but as the initiative had the support of the Principal, work began.

The teaching, as at Birmingham, was done by academics with particular interests in industry. The first Dean, Sydney Chapman, was from a business family, and had written on the Lancashire cotton industry and work and wages. The staff were helped by numbers of businessmen combining teaching with a business career, in accounting, banking, railway transport and the cotton industry. The Manchester programme tended more towards economics and less towards the management of firms than Birmingham's. It consisted of general economics, economic geography, modern history, languages, science subjects, the structure of industry, accounting, and commercial law. There were special subjects, for example, a course on the cotton industry, and one on the very topical law of patents, designs, and trade marks. The programme was aimed not only at the favoured few who could attend daytime classes and had a position waiting for them, but young men who, already employed, were prepared to attend classes in the evenings. As the Faculty of Law at Manchester offered evening degrees for articled clerks, so the Faculty of Commerce determined to offer classes after office hours for clerks in business firms. Examinations were arranged as far as possible at times of the year convenient for local businesses. As an added incentive to evening students, they were allowed to pass in one subject at a time.

The number of students enrolling was satisfactory, and rose

steadily – from fifteen in the first year to fifty-six in 1913. But the funds of the original appeal were nearly exhausted by 1911 and the university looked for a permanent endowment for the faculty. Attempts to attract more funds from Manchester businesses brought in some scholarships, but very little more before the First World War. There was a great upsurge in student enrolments after the war, and a separate Chair of Commerce was approved. But as fees and other income did not cover expenses, the Faculty remained in dire financial difficulties. There were a few very welcome items of income during the inter-war years. In 1922, Lewis's Ltd, the Manchester department stores group, gave £3,000 for postgraduate study into industry and commerce and for an economics library.[20] (Its chairman, F. J. Marquis, who later became Lord Woolton, had studied economics under Chapman.) In the late 1920s the Faculty received a bequest of £10,000 'for the development of higher commercial education', and £4,000 for the foundation of commercial scholarships. There were other small sums towards staffing and scholarships. In 1931, the government commissioned an industrial survey of Lancashire. The research group on this project continued together and it attracted funds, although primarily from American bodies, not British businesses. The Rockefeller Foundation made grants of $5,000 in 1934 and then $20,000 over five years; the United States' Social Science Research Council gave £3,500 for an enquiry into Public Administration in 1937. The Manchester cotton trade, as an exception, spent £700 a year from 1936 on research into wages and labour.

Manchester has always been regarded as a well-supported university, but it was not so well supported that it could aid the Faculty of Commerce to any extent. In 1920 the financial position of the University was causing great anxiety. The University Council hoped that 'the work of the University will not be impeded by want of support from the great industrial area it primarily serves'.[21] A public appeal for £500,000 to help extinguish a debt of £130,000 and make improvements raised £232,000 over the next two years. The University Grants Committee assisted with £20,000 and an increased annual grant, but an adverse balance remained until 1930 when it was dissolved with government aid.

Businessmen well understood that without their support a business degree could not develop, and they chose not to contribute financially. But more importantly, they did not seek to recruit the graduates. Employers were not persuaded that the graduates of the faculty had anything to offer to the business world. As late as 1944 the Manchester appointments board was being told that men and women who had taken an arts or commerce degree had wasted their time.[22]

The numbers of students enrolling had continued to grow satisfactorily after the First World War, and the non-degree work was still attracting large classes. But the business degree was now giving cause for concern. Over half the degrees were evening degrees, and a high proportion of people taking them did not have a business career in mind. They were teachers, Civil Servants, and clerks with little hope of promotion, taking the opportunity to gain a university degree by evening study. In the mid-1920s the faculty made a reassessment of its work given the continuing low business demand for commerce graduates. Economics and administration were upgraded in the syllabus, commerce downgraded. Modifications were made to the degree to allow students to take more courses relevant to public administration. Then separate degrees were instituted – the B.A.(Com.) and the B.A.(Admin.). Enrolments for the latter began to grow, at the expense of the former. By 1935 more students were enrolling for administration than for commerce. The Chair of Commerce had already been suspended. In 1943 it was resolved that the name of the faculty be changed from Commerce and Administration to Economic and Social Science, a name more appropriate to 'the present development of many of the subjects with which the Faculty is concerned'.[23] And in the late 1950s the Bachelor of Commerce degree began to be phased out.

Before the First World War, and for a few years afterwards, both Birmingham and Manchester had retained some hope that British businessmen would become interested in business education and support their efforts to develop an appropriate programme. They had not had much success before 1914, but just after the war it did seem that business interest was about to be kindled. Conditions in 1919–20 looked so promising, especially in the area of industrial relations, that there were even attempts in the private sector to offer an educational service to management. The Institute of Industrial Administration was set up, and offered to produce a 'professional' manager who would act as a third force between capital and labour. The new National Institute of Industrial Psychology offered consulting services on matters relating to personnel and efficiency questions. Then Seebohm Rowntree, of the cocoa firm at York, as an expression of his concern for industrial relations and business efficiency, instituted the Oxford Management Conferences for foremen. The London School of Economics had also decided by this time that the signs were sufficiently propitious to justify making a second attempt at a business degree.

London: the Commerce Degree

This second effort by Sidney Webb at the LSE began, in the British context at least, with a significant amount of business interest. Industry between 1917 and 1920 contributed financial support and advice on the curriculum in impressive amounts. Sir Ernest Cassel's educational trust (of which Webb was a trustee) put up £150,000 in War Loan providing £7,500 a year, and an appeal was launched by a group of businessmen to match the Cassel figure. By the end of 1919, £120,000 had been promised. Much of this was from financial institutions, shipping, and large retail stores, but many other firms contributed small amounts. There were a number of scholarships – one at £2,000, four at £250, two at £150, and five at £90. Nine groups of businessmen formed themselves into committees to advise on what should be taught. They submitted between them detailed reports on higher commercial education for Banking, Australasian Trade, Distributing, Eastern Trade, Engineering, Non-Ferrous Metals, Printing, Publishing, and Newspaper Trades, Shipping, and Inland Transport.[24] The new degree was to be made available both to day and evening students, and a Commerce Degree Bureau set up to give guidance to external B.Com. students and to bring graduates and prospective employers together.

The published syllabus was broadly similar to Ashley's at Birmingham – two years of a broad but relevant education, and a third year which was more directly vocational. In the third year LSE students could choose one from nine groups of subjects to fit in with their chosen career: Banking and Finance, Trade I, Trade II (an area course), Industry, General Transport, Shipping, Inland Transport, Public Utilities, and Commercial Art. (Commercial Art had been included in response to the current criticisms of British design capabilities.)

The new director of the LSE, the young and politically astute

William Beveridge, had decided to give this initiative his backing, and there was no shortage of publicity. The King laid the foundation stone of the new building for 'teaching Commerce for the Commercial Degrees of the University of London'.[25] The initiative gained overall a good reception, and student numbers were immediately satisfactory: eighty-nine full-time students registered for the new B.Com. degree in the first year. Unfortunately, graduates with the new degree found themselves in the early 1920s emerging into a job market which had almost dried up. The sudden and deep depression had overwhelmed any earlier enthusiasm employers might have had for graduates in commerce. The first graduates were helped into positions in the City by the School's governors, and it was hoped that they would 'prove their worth and the value of their training, and will make it continually more easy for fresh generations of Commerce graduates to follow them'.[26]

The level of business enthusiasm over the next two decades demonstrated that the new degree had not engendered a new demand. The B.Com. graduate was no more sought after than any other graduate. In 1924 the London Chamber of Commerce reminded the School that

The great majority of employers are not anxious to employ University men or women. They prefer to recruit their staff at the age of sixteen or seventeen, as in most cases actual experience of office routine is more valuable to the employer than general commercial knowledge. Any responsible posts which cannot be filled by the promotion of men or women already on the staff, are given to applicants with business experience ... .

While there can be no doubt that the Bachelor of Commerce has a good general background for business work, it is of little value to the employer until a man has had some practical experience. Business men have to be educated to appreciate the possibilities in employing graduates.[27]

Some firms in the 1920s and 1930s, such as the Gas Light and Coke Company, Harrods, and some of the banks, expressed the view that the new degree was a good thing. However, neither they nor any other firm now considered it to be such a good thing that they would seek to recruit new men with the degree. They were prepared to encourage their staffs to take the evening degree, and the banks in particular had many B.Com. graduates who had gained their degree by evening study. Over a quarter of the LSE's evening B.Com. students were bank clerks in the 1920s, although the degree carried little weight for promotion with the banks.

Some ten years after its inception a question-mark arose over the future of this determined and very hopeful venture into business education. The annual output of B.Com. graduates had remained at a satisfactory level – peaking at fifty-nine in 1934 – but the degree was hardly fulfilling the role originally allotted to it. The graduates were, on the whole, in business, but business had not demanded them. Of a sample of 201 LSE commerce graduates in 1932, 116 were evening students and of these seventy-two were already in business occupations when they enrolled. Of the remaining eighty-five (day) students in the sample, forty-eight had gone into business occupations, the remainder being spread over government service, further study, teaching, and other professions.[28] In 1931 the B.Com. was given a common syllabus for the first two years with the B.Sc.(Econ.). In 1932 it was found that a lower proportion of commerce students had graduated than economic students: the cause was believed to be a lower quality of student selecting to study commerce. A report for the University of London in 1935 suggested that the B.Com. could not justify its separate existence. The School's director, William Beveridge, did not agree, arguing that the funds had been donated for the specific purpose of supporting the B.Com. degree, and that the appeal had resulted in 'the bringing to the University of large support from the City for the first time in recent history'.[29] After Beveridge's departure in 1937, however, and the acute pressures on staff and accommodation after the Second World War, the B.Com. was absorbed into the B.Sc.(Econ.). The Federation of British Industries had advised in 1947 that, in its view, 'a B.Comm. course is not appropriate for full-time University study, and that the possession of a B.Comm. degree can hardly be regarded as a qualification of significant value for entry into industry'. Industry would, the FBI thought, for the most part prefer to recruit a B.Sc.(Econ.) rather than a B.Com.[30] It was no longer offered at the LSE after 1949.

The University of London had been prepared to institute the degree. The energetic William Beveridge had been prepared to direct it. Students had been prepared to spend their own time and money in gaining it, to some extent as an investment in their future. A sample survey of 175 LSE commerce graduates undertaken in the early 1980s revealed that some 60 per cent had chosen to read commerce as a means of improving their chances in business. They reported that it had provided them with skills and a depth of understanding of the business world which they believed were valuable in their work.[31] But British industry had not been prepared to play its part and recruit the graduates. Without a reasonable level of demand, the subject could not be developed and the supply of graduates could not continue to be produced for very long.

A frequent criticism of the commerce degree was that it was all too theoretical, and what business wanted was men with more practical knowledge. But practical knowledge required the practical co-operation of firms, and this was not forthcoming. An earlier hope of the new universities had been that academic study and practical experience would be combined in the new degree. The analogy with the medical student was not thought to be too unrealistic: visits to firms, talks by managers, vacation work, research projects, were all thought to be possible, and very necessary for future businessmen. There had been some little success in making contact with firms, but the ties were not strong.

A widespread belief, in academe as well as in the business world, was that it was not possible, even with the co-operation of industry, for academics to succeed with a business degree. This belief prompted a rather different approach by a group of businessmen in Manchester. In 1918 six business leaders – all from progressive manufacturing and textile firms – decided that, with their involvement, higher education could help to train industry's future leaders.

Manchester: the Department of Industrial Administration

In 1918 six businessmen joined with the Principal of the Manchester Municipal School of Technology to set up a department which offered industrial administration subjects to men already in or about to enter manufacturing industry. The institution already offered technical subjects at all levels, from apprentice to undergraduate. The six businessmen were looking for ways to increase business efficiency but at the same time improve industrial relations in manufacturing. They believed that if the next generation of British managers were educated in the principles of 'scientific management' tempered, however, with the findings of the emerging disciplines of physiology and psychology, productivity must be raised and industrial peace ensured. The 'human factor' in business was not to be – could not be, they argued – ignored in the drive for efficiency. They appointed as the first director of the new department not an economist but a professor of physiology, then at Bristol University. To ensure that the teaching was sufficiently practical, an experienced works manager/lecturer in mechanical engineering was appointed as his second-in-command.

The aim of Manchester's Department of Industrial Administration was to provide training in all aspects of industrial management, for all levels in the managerial hierarchy – from foreman to works director – during both daytime and evenings. The organising committee identified three main areas of study: background subjects such as economics and history, then works and company management, and finally man management. The vice-principal of the college offered to teach the background subjects, and a young ex-businessman, J. Bowie, joined them to teach economics and commerce.

The Department opened for teaching with an intake of British and foreign ex-servicemen: these were being funded by government for short, intensive courses in industrial administration to prepare them for civilian employment. The Vice-Principal explained to Bowie that 'We want especially to get them interested in modern movements in industry – to discuss the Whitley Reports, Works Committees, Trade Union organisation at the present time, the Shop Stewards movement, Guild Socialism, and present currents of thought.'[32] The Department was soon teaching a wide range of subjects which it put under the heading of industrial administration, and which attracted primarily technical men. There were lectures on the organisation of labour, fatigue, welfare, time and motion study, and industrial hygiene; works design, cost accounting, plant and storage problems, and the law of insurance. In 1921 it, very ambitiously, offered a full-time course in Industrial Administration, another in Industrial and Social Work, plus part-time day and evening courses in industrial administration for the School's own certificates and diplomas.

The Department had begun as a five-year experiment, and it was agreed that it had got off to a good start. But the depression then hit the DIA's progress very sharply, as it did all the other post-

1918 educational initiatives. The professor of physiology had also proved to be a wrong choice. But the main drawback was the department's continuing lack of adequate financing. Its original funding had been minimal. The six businessmen had each agreed to contribute £150 a year for five years, and to invite six others to join them on the committee for an equal sum. They could not persuade six others to join. An appeal to local companies for fifteen subscriptions of £100 per annum was not reached, and some companies withdrew after they had made an agreement. In 1923, for example, Metropolitan Vickers withdrew its subscription 'for reasons of economy'.[33] Another appeal for five guineas a year was not a success. The Manchester Education Committee then offered a maximum of £900 per annum if the rest could be found from outside subscribers. In 1926, the Education Committee agreed to assume full responsibility for the maintenance of the department.

At this time, Manchester University was looking into the subject of industrial administration as a subject of university study. They approved it, 'in addition to and not in substitution for' the courses they already offered for the B.Com. In 1927 the DIA was recognised as a Department of the Faculty of Technology. Industrial administration subjects were to form part of the B.Sc.Tech. degree syllabus and part of the postgraduate degree courses. One-year full-time postgraduate and two-year full-time, non-university, certificated courses were planned. The emphasis was very much on subjects relevant to manufacturing industry, and for the post-graduate course the stated intention was to emphasise administration. To this end, various new subjects were introduced – industrial output, purchasing and stock control, wage systems, business statistics, and factory costing. There were plans to visit local businesses in order to study business activity on-site and so help students 'develop a sound practical attitude to business problems'. The Director reported that the department used the practical Case Method of teaching (pioneered by Harvard Business School) wherever possible, although his judgement was that it had to be used with caution. In 1930, the Director visited the United States to gain more experience of American business schools.

There were always good attendance levels at the evening classes and part-time day classes, and some firms paid for short-term training for their foremen-level staff. The Bleachers' and Dyers'

Association, for example, sent fifteen students to attend the whole of the Wednesday morning course. The response to the full-time courses was much less satisfactory. In 1928 there were eight full-time men students, and they were not local men. The highest number of full-time day students in the department reached only twenty-one, in 1938. In that year the DIA attempted another scheme to interest Manchester employers. This scheme allowed a firm to choose and sponsor a good man. The business committee wrote to employers, explaining that the department 'had as its object the development of suitable courses for students ... who might be expected to provide industry with trained material for future managerial positions'.[34]

In 1944, in the discussions on the future of the DIA, it was admitted that 'there is much work to be done in convincing the heads of industrial undertakings in the region which the College serves of the utility of the study of the whole field of Industrial Administration'.

The new director believed that since 'We are concerned with the functions of forecasting, planning, organising, directing, co-ordinating, and controlling a concern',[35] the department should offer a full degree course in industrial administration. He called a meeting of leading local industrialists to ask their views. The industrialists advised that there was not now, and would not be in the future, any demand for degrees or diplomas in industrial administration. They preferred the subjects to be supplementary to technical training and taken in evening classes or short full-time courses. Charles Renold, a businessman who had been on the original committee of six, thought differently. While admitting that

Twenty–five years of experience of the Department has shown that whilst it has achieved considerable success with the lower grades of management and administration, it has not made any very significant impact on the problems either of developing the art and science of higher management or of training for industrial leadership at the higher levels,[36]

he advocated expansion, with a Graduate School and a Research Bureau. There were in 1945 in the department only three full-time staff and fifteen part-time lecturers. The teaching load was such that no research was possible. Renold compared this with Harvard

University business school's thirty-two full Professors, thirty-nine Assistants, six Administration Officers, and a Research Division employing three full-time Directors of Research and their staffs. He drafted a Degree of Bachelor of Technical Sciences in Industrial Administration. Manchester industrialists were certain, however, that they preferred evening classes and part-time study taken on the student's own initiative.

The meeting with industrialists did produce one supportive suggestion – that of a lecture-discussion group for senior executives. This was regarded later as having been highly successful from its inception, and very useful for advertising the Department's facilities. It was still felt that local industry was largely unaware of the training the Department offered. There was, too, in the post-1945 period a pressing need for the quality and quantity of the Department's work to be acknowledged. From the early 1940s government had taken a lively interest in the management of British industry and set in motion various committees to advise it on how, if at all, the capacities of those in management could be improved. The 1945 Percy Committee on Higher Technological Education drew attention to the importance of the subjects of industrial administration, and favoured establishing a centre of research and training in business management. This would feed trained teaching staff into educational establishments, as well as relevantly educated and trained managers into British industry. Soon afterwards, the Baillieu Committee reported in favour of a British Institute of Management which would, among other things, 'co-operate in the development of training and educational schemes for management ... aim to raise the standards of management throughout the country and maintain them at high level ... and help to create in industry and commerce a continuous supply of good managers'.[37] Then the Urwick Committee (1947) recommended establishing national professional qualifications for business management. The director of the DIA felt in 1952 that 'It is almost inevitable that a great movement is beginning', and that the claim of the Department of Industrial Administration in the University of Manchester to become *the* centre mentioned in the Percy Report was a very strong one. He then put forward the idea of a course which would include practical training in industrial establishments during the months of July to October. It would be, he thought, 'analogous to that given as training for the practice of medicine wherein students walk the wards (in the field of IA, workshops or offices) before formally entering the profession as qualified men'.[38] He also pressed for the one-year postgraduate course to be extended to two years.

The main competitor for the prize of *the* centre of teaching and research was thought to be the LSE's Department of Business Administration. Despite the earlier rebuffs from business, the School had tried yet again, in 1930, to interest British businessmen in formal education for business management.

London: the Department of Business Administration

As at Manchester, London's department of business administration was initiated by a small group of businessmen, all noted for their interest in modern management methods. The London people were members of existing management associations, including the recently-formed Management Research Groups,[39] and two of them were practising accountants who also taught at the LSE. They had decided that modern management would benefit from the research and teaching skills, and the status, attached to a university.

In 1928 they had begun preparing a draft scheme for research and training on 'those definite problems which arise in the course of management activities and are common to all businesses' as a combined operation between the School and business. The draft scheme noted that 'the teaching of Business Administration is only possible if based upon research',[40] and it proposed the setting-up of a small semi-independent research department to gather and prepare material which would then be used in a programme of training for business administration. The proposers thought that 'If the experiment were successful it might at a later stage be advisable to seek the full recognition of London University in the form of the institution of a Diploma in Industrial Administration.' The students were all to have had at least two years' business experience: later the department might be willing to consider a pre-experience postgraduate course. A departmental committee of businessmen and academics would between them choose from the applicants men who had 'those qualities of personality and character which would be likely to presage development into a successful and competent business executive'. After some initial hesitation, William Beveridge received the proposal of a small research department and a director, a deputy, and three research assistants, favourably. The Railway Research Service was already being run successfully, and business research bureaux were proving very successful in American universities not only at forwarding the study of business administration but also of economic science. Beveridge, with his intense interest in 'realistic economics', was very attracted to the idea of such a bureau under his control.

An appeals committee gained the moral support of a number of prominent men of affairs. However, try as it might, it could not persuade firms to fund the venture generously. ICI and Lord Waring (of Waring and Gillow, the London-based furniture store group) were persuaded to subscribe £500 per annum, but still the minimum required sum of £5,000 a year for five years could not be reached. After much acrimonious debate, with a final sum of £4,500 a year promised and the services of a Principal squeezed from the LSE, the project was launched. The first year, 1930, was spent in preparation. The department's staff studied the new business school in Paris (the Centre de Préparation aux Affaires) which had been financed by the Paris Chamber of Commerce. The head of the department, Jules Menken (an American and a consulting economist), went to America to learn from their experiences. The Dean of Harvard's business school visited Beveridge and offered his co-operation with the new venture. As a result of this visit, Harvard loaned one of its professors of marketing to assist with the department's teaching of marketing for one term. Harvard's volumes of business problems ('cases') were made available. Menken took up the Case Method (essentially, an unguided group discussion of management problems drawn from actual business experience) with enthusiasm, and expected that British firms would make similar case material available, since these would be more relevant to the British trainee executive.

The scheme was advertised as a two-year, full-time course (as at Harvard), with exemptions available for the first year, and the possibility of taking the first year by evening study alone.

The first year is intended to give students a general background of economics, statistics, accounting, commercial law and other subjects, essential to profitable specialised study of business. The second year is designed to give students a thorough understanding of marketing, production and finance – the three major divisions of business; to equip them with an adequate knowledge of statistics and accounting as instruments of executive control; and to familiarise them with the main problems of personnel management.[41]

Although the student body was initially expected to be twenty young executives released by their firms, this was found not to produce many students. The rule was amended the following year to include new graduates judged by the Selection Committee to be suitable for business careers. To encourage firms to send their young executives a scheme of subscriptions was launched – firms subscribing £50 a year would be allowed remission or rebate of the normal fees. Twenty-nine firms, most of which were already interested in university training and/or education for business management, subscribed in this way. However, only a few of them sent their young staff on the course. During the first four years of teaching, nine firms sent sixteen students for the second of the two years. But not all of the firms were sending their best men, and not all were satisfied with the arrangements. The firms had considered two years to be entirely too long, but the young executives were not always equipped with sufficient economics and accounting to go straight on to the second year. The ICI contact complained, 'I think there will always be difficulty in finding candidates who have actually taken an Economics Degree, since men who have that qualification are not necessarily those whom we judge to be future executives ... .'[42] ICI chose to withdraw from the scheme rather than allow its men two years or make sure that its future executives had a background knowledge of economics, statistics, and accounting.

The numbers being nominated by firms were many fewer than had been hoped, but Beveridge had become enamoured of the idea of the department as a 'staff college' and was reluctant to close the door on the scheme to nominate students. He wrote in 1934 that, 'Though I myself am far from being convinced that the staff college idea will prove permanently practicable, it might be worth keeping alive as a means of attracting money. It is going to be exceedingly difficult to get the Department endowed by subscriptions given for the general good.'[43] The total numbers enrolling from all sources were also fewer than hoped for. This prompted another idea, the University Scheme. With the aid of the university appointments boards, firms were to select graduates and offer them a post, to be taken up on the satisfactory completion of the Department's course. The graduate paid all the costs of the course, and the business post was probationary for one year. The numbers increased as a result of the scheme (to twenty-eight in 1933 and twenty-six in 1934), but unfortunately for the department, the important Cambridge University appointments board could not be persuaded to join in.

In 1934, after four years of the five-year experiment, Beveridge asked for confidential reports from three different sources. Menken produced a report. 'This course has not been perfect', he wrote.

Lack of funds and staff compelled much teaching which should have broken new ground to be done during these years on conventional lines. New methods and new material were used chiefly in the organisation of Factory Visits and Business Discussions, to some extent in the teaching of Statistics, but above all in the Marketing Courses. Here all the material used and all the problems treated have been gathered fresh from current business practice; teaching has throughout been based on the Case Method.[44]

He advocated a large expansion of resources. Beveridge was not amused. To add to the DBA's troubles, there was a growing struggle in the Department broadly between the normal university staff on the one side and Menken and the businessmen on the other. The report from the businessman Lord Piercy advised Beveridge that 'The impression which the Department makes on the students is a good one. They are interested, keen, and on the whole feel they are receiving a training which will help them ... .' But there were weaknesses, not least of which was the lack of clarity of the actual aims of the course:

It is clear that the Department aims at giving something analogous to a vocational training for Business, that is, at turning out students with a general idea of what they are likely to find in business, what they are likely to be expected to do, and how, in a general way, to take hold of it. Along this line of thought, the particular function of the Department would be, I suggest, to concentrate on business practice, and the subject matter of its teaching would be rather the descriptive analysis of certain main fields of business administration, with a view to the formulation of current systems of operation, rules of practice and the like, than the economic analysis of business.[45]

The Department, he suggested, had to come down firmly on one side or the other. The university staff concentrated their teaching on the economic analysis of business, while Menken supported the analysis of business practice. Beveridge decided he wanted tighter control. He took the advice of the Professor of Commerce who suggested that a re-structured DBA be fully integrated into the School. In 1935 the businessmen and Menken departed. The new Department, under the Professor of Commerce, took over the other business administration work carried on in other departments in the School, and offered from 1935 a one-year postgraduate course in business administration. The visits to firms and the seminars with businessmen continued, but now there was 'an appropriate balance of general principles'.

The number of students the new course attracted – around twenty – was satisfactory. There were bursaries to be had, and the course could be taken as one year of an undergraduate or postgraduate degree. The departmental funding, however, was causing great concern, even though costs were being pared to the bone (the School had demanded that costs did not exceed £1,500 a year).[46] An appeal launched in 1937 for a capital fund of £100,000 to produce £3,500 a year had produced less than £5,000 two years later. Business had clearly indicated that it was not interested in funding the LSE's attempt at business administration, nor moreover was it particularly interested in employing the graduates of the Department. Over two-thirds of them went into business occupations, but they seem not to have enhanced their chances of being offered a good position to any significant extent. Industrial demand, Menken had judged, would need a great deal of hard work to develop, but, whatever hard work had been expended, by the onset of the Second World War the development had been slight.

The DBA closed in 1939 for the duration of the war. Professor Arnold Plant, still the head of the Department, was anxious for it to reopen as soon as possible in order to benefit from the new developments the government was initiating. He argued that the Department would benefit from close collaboration with the proposed Central (British) Institute of Management, 'by strengthening the ties with business firms, practising managers, research and management associations throughout the country, and in that way ensure the continuing appreciation of business developments and needs'.[47] It reopened in 1948.

In 1950, the University attracted £35,000 from Great Universal Stores (the mail order distributors) to establish ten scholarships in business administration and £1,500 annually for research.[48] But despite the better links the Department was now establishing with firms, and its endeavours to find a major role for itself in the government's new plans for management education, it remained a small-scale project. In 1961 not all the twenty-five places were filled, and only eight of the students were British. Its work was finally transferred to other departments in 1965.

Most of the other civic universities had offered a business training along similar lines to those described above, but none had any great success. The older universities had all the while kept themselves informed on the developments in business education, and they had not considered it necessary to initiate a scheme, at least until the 1950s. The University of Cambridge appointments board had had a second look at business training after Beveridge had begun to look successful in the early 1930s. It set up a committee under Dr Will Spens to research the whole question of a preparatory training for Cambridge graduates entering business. This committee looked first at the United States. It asked advice of Columbia University, Yale, and Harvard, and it sent two of its younger members to look at the Case Method in operation. It also had the benefit of research carried out on its behalf by Lever Brothers in the States. A sub-committee was set up to advise 'on the provision of a course of study at Cambridge for men who intend to adopt a business career'. This sub-committee devised a scheme of business training as an option in the economics degree – but the discussions had not been concluded before the war intervened. After the war, the improving conditions for the universities reduced any immediate need to initiate schemes of business education, and there was no need now to consider anything of the sort at undergraduate level. In the 1950s, the appointments boards of both Oxford and Cambridge responded to the changing mood and offered an educational service, connected with but not part of the University, for men in senior management. They were short courses, and they were well attended.

The earlier rejection of business education by Oxford and Cambridge had had its effect on the initiatives in the new universities. Their influence had not only helped to keep the liberal arts tradition strong, by acting as a deterrent to the most able students and academics to enter into business-related studies, but it had affected the views of business leaders on the subject. There was, quite naturally, competition between the universities for the ear of employers and for the posts which were suitable for university graduates, whatever sector the posts were in. The Oxford appointments board was not very effective in pushing Oxford men, and according to its own account, at one stage seemed 'to act like a fly-paper' in attracting to its books 'men who are either too old, or have failed in other callings, or younger men whom it would be difficult to recommend with confidence for any post'.[49] But the appointments board at Cambridge became very adept at getting opportunities for Cambridge graduates. The board had the resources to allow frequent visits to firms, and it encouraged older graduates to visit the board to discuss their own position and prospects and any possible openings for more Cambridge graduates. Prospective employers were persuaded by the board variously to change the date of their entrance examinations, and the content of the examination papers, to suit Cambridge candidates better.[50] It offered employers advice on what starting salary to offer, the conditions of employment, and the necessity for some sort of training for new men. No other appointments board was nearly so effective as that at Cambridge. However, the board also used its position to influence business against supporting business education in the universities. While the board had no doubt that an Oxbridge education best fitted a man for a business career, the business graduate was a challenge, and the board members met the challenge whenever occasion permitted. Their antipathy to university business training was transmitted directly by the board's staff on their visits to firms. It was also transmitted to employers by influential businessmen, like Waley Cohen of Shell, co-opted to the board. The Oxford board was 'publicly hostile to commerce and even economics education for industry as being useless'.[51]

Those British directors of large firms who had decided that the arts man rather than a man with a relevant education from the new universities was more appropriate management material for their companies, did not come to their decision solely on the advice of the ancient universities. They did, however, choose the one without trying the other. The choice was crucial for business education. The business graduate had to be taken up by the large firm if the business degree were to gain any credibility as a preparation for management. But with his specialists trained to cover the technical aspects of the firm, and the arts man chosen to play the part of the 'generalist', the leading British firms felt little need of the man with a scholastic training in business. The Oxbridge influence in the Boards of the largest companies in the country was a drawback that these early attempts at management education could not afford.

References

1 W. Barnes, *Managerial Catalyst: the Story of London Business School 1964 to 1989*, Paul Chapman, 1989, p. 6.

2 Federation of British Industries, *Bulletin*, 19 May 1919, p. 250.

3 *Economic Journal*, March 1904, p. 88.

4 *Economic Journal*, June 1902, p. 227.

5 *Economica*, I, January 1921, p. 13.

6 Sir Sydney Caine, *The History of the Foundation of the London School of Economics and Political Science*, G. Bell, p. 43.

7 *Sphere*, 30 January 1909.

8 M. Sanderson, *The Universities and British Industry 1850–1970*, Routledge and Kegan Paul, 1972, p. 193.

9 B. M. D. Smith, 'Education for management: its conception and implementation in the Faculty of Commerce at Birmingham', unpublished paper, University of Birmingham, May 1974, p. 12.

10 Smith, 'Education for management', p. 8.

11 Smith, 'Education for management', p. 18.

12 (Sir) W.J. Ashley, *Commercial Education*, Williams and Norgate, 1926, pp. 62–5.

13 Royal Commission on the Civil Service. 1914. *Appendix to the Fifth Report of the Commissioners*, Minutes of Evidence. W. J. Ashley, Q.43,596, 10 July 1914.

14 Smith, 'Education for management', p. 29.

15 S. P. Keeble, 'University education and business management from the 1890s to the 1950s: a reluctant relationship', unpublished London Ph.D. thesis, January 1984, p. 39.

16 Quoted in Smith, 'Education for management', p. 30.

17 University of Birmingham (UB), Report of the Principal to the Council, 1922–23, p. 7.

18 UB, Report of the Principal to the Council, 1925–26, p. 18.

19 The Manchester Chamber of Commerce, *Monthly Record*, 31 March 1902.

20 University of Manchester (UM), Report of the Council to the Court of Governors, 1922–24, ref. UA/23.

21 UM, Report of the Council to the Court of Governors, November 1920, UA/23.

22 UM Appointments Board Council Minutes, 8 May 1944.

23 UM Faculty of Economics and Social Science, Minute 25 October 1943, 7 December 1943.

24 University of London (UL), Minutes of Senate 1918–19, available in UL Senate House Library.

25 UL Senate Minute 2725, 18 May 1920.

26 London School of Economics (LSE), Report on the teaching of commerce, June 1924, p. 1, Commerce Committee 1924–28.

27 LSE, Pearson, 'Report', interview 52.

28 LSE, *Register 1895–1932*, March 1934.

29 UL Minutes of Senate, SM 658, 16 November 1938, Appendix AC11, AC12.

30 FBI, Memorandum 22 April 1947, Education Committee Minutes, File 116.

31 Keeble, 'University education', pp. 253f.

32 University of Manchester Institute of Science and Technology (UMIST), memorandum 25 February 1919, File: Bowie E59.

33 UMIST, DIA, Minutes 24 July 1918 – 30 October 1923, File: Industrial Administration.

34 UMIST, DIA, letter to employers, 25 January 1938, File F4: Industrial Administration, June 1937 – December 1947.

35 UMIST, DIA, memorandum 12 May 1945, File F4.

36 UMIST, DIA, memorandum 19 June 1946, File F4.

37 Quoted in UMIST, DIA Director's Report, 16 May 1946.

38 UMIST, DIA, Report of the Director, 16 May 1946, File F4.

39 The Management Research Groups are described in S. P. Keeble, 'Management Research Groups', *Business Archives*, November 1981.

40 LSE, 'Draft scheme for a course in business administration proposed for the consideration of the LSE', 1928, DBA File 196A.

41 LSE, DBA pamphlet 'Training for business management', 1931, p. 7.

42 LSE, Letter from Sir Frank Spickernell, ICI, to W. H. Beveridge, 8 October 1931, File: DBA 196D.

43 LSE, Note from W. H. Beveridge to J. Menken, 20 June 1934, File: DBA 196E.

44 LSE, Report on the first four years, File: DBA 196E.

45 LSE, Report by W. Piercy, File 196E, 1932–34.

46 LSE, Professorial Council, 17 November 1937, p. 4, File: DBA

196G 1937–46.

47 LSE, Note from A. Plant to L. Farrer Brown, File 196G, 1937–46.

48 *Universities Yearbook*, 1953, p. 197.

49 F. B. Hunt and C. E. Escritt, 'Historical notes on the Oxford University Appointments Committee, 1892–1950', unpublished typescript, 1951, p. 5.

50 University of Cambridge Appointments Board, Employers' Visits, 29 March 1935, 8 November 1938, 27 July 1939.

51 Sanderson, *The Universities*, p. 271.

Chapter 6

The rejection of planned experience

What British employers traditionally wanted in the men they appointed was sufficient experience to do the job on hand, no more and no less. Firms filled vacant posts with men who knew, or could get to know after some on-the-job instruction, how an individual job was being done and were capable of taking it on. They looked for men to serve the job, not men with ability whose capacities might be developed to serve the company in the longer term. Men with sufficient experience could be recruited from outside the firm or department or promoted from within.

A man interested in developing his own abilities through experience in different firms, different industries, or different functions, found it increasingly difficult to do so as the twentieth century progressed. He was made aware that not many firms of any size would be impressed. Thoughts of disloyalty, an inability to settle down, and overweening ambition, were likely to arise in the firm or department he wanted to leave *and* the firm or department he wanted to join. Some firms placed strong obstacles in the way of a man leaving. He could be pressed to sign a long-term contract, to prevent his moving. This could happen even where there was no question of a man having technical knowledge of use to a competitor. It was argued in 1928 that 'there are too many enterprises in which the transfer of any member of the executive staff is regarded as a disloyal act to be hampered or prevented by long-term agreements, limiting the freedom of the officer concerned in seeking any kind of alternative employment'.[1] One Cambridge graduate in 1939 had signed a contract to serve his company until he was sixty-five years old: he was thirty-five when he signed.[2] Some men also had to contend with the existence of employer poaching agreements. The new firm would not take on a man without 'consultation' with the old firm. In Standard Telephones and Cables this type of arrangement lasted well into the 1960s. It was reported of this firm, too, as of many others, that barriers were placed on men attempting to move within the company. 'There were instances of division managers refusing to let people go and the only way they were able to transfer was to leave and spend some time with another company before coming back.'[3] There was the knowledge, too, that any pension rights would be lost in the move, and most appointments demanded a probationary period which he might or might not survive.

Aspiring managers depended very much, therefore, on the firm they joined being able and willing to offer continuing opportunities. University graduates in particular hoped for a good introductory training, and opportunities for periods of learning in other departments and branches, preferably related to career moves in the organisation. They believed, as did some elements in ICI, that 'if leaders of high quality are to be trained for the future, it is essential that the most promising men should be given wide experience by movement from job to job and should be trained in responsibility by rapid experience *during their formative years*'.[4] In the 1930s planned experience was seen to be of particular value in large firms. 'Training by Systematic Variation of Experience', it was argued, 'is certainly one means by which the present tendency to extreme specialization may be to some extent overcome.'[5]

The major task for manufacturing industry in the first half of the century was that of preparing the technical man for higher management. Technical men were needed at the highest levels to give senior management's decision-making the advantage of input from engineering and scientific sources, and to counterbalance the influence of the accountants and marketing men. Monck made the point in 1952 that 'an accountant can get wider experience than the engineer without incurring the odium of changing jobs too often'.[6] The technical staff were also a major source of potentially able men for future management posts: successful foreign manufacturing enterprises were using their technical men as managers to very good effect. And production needed to be signposted much more clearly as a route into management in order to attract good quality recruits to manufacturing. While there were large numbers of managers in British firms who were technical men, they were not fairly represented at the highest levels. The study by Monck of the boards of 725 public companies in the engineering industry found that over two-thirds of the 'self-selecting aristocracy of some 4,000 strong' were without technical qualifications.[7] And they were normally ill-prepared to move into managerial positions. Yet the efforts made to upgrade and develop the technical man through programmes of experience-based learning were very meagre on any measurement, even by the best British firms.

Some managements needed to adjust their own attitudes. They saw men with an engineering or science training as, at best, technical managers, not top executives or members of the board. Tootal Broadhurst and Lee, a firm proud of its thoroughgoing schemes for technical men by the mid-1920s, saw its brightest men as potential mill managers. 'Youths approaching eighteen or twenty years of age', the firm reported,

who show promise of special ability in technical knowledge and of skill at work are given experience in different departments of the mill, with close contact with overlookers and foremen in the discharge of their duties. They are gradually promoted to more responsible work as their fitness improves and when opportunity occurs. These promotions gradually lead to positions as overlookers, from which selections are usually made for appointment as under-managers and managers.[8]

The scheme produced experienced and reliable mill managers. On the other hand, the efforts had little effect on the company's emerging problem of a paucity of good men above that level. In this and other firms, if technical men did find themselves promoted into senior posts which required wide-ranging business skills, they discovered at that stage their ability (or lack of it) to handle the work.

The Metropolitan-Vickers Electrical Company – a firm with American roots, and one strongly committed to new technology and in-company training – was one firm which, by the mid-1930s, was offering technical men a wider understanding of the business enterprise and the possibility of a career in other functions. One of its founding companies, British Westinghouse, had begun a fine record of training on the technical side before the First World War. In 1911 two-year courses were being offered to young men having B.Sc. or equivalent degrees: there was no premium demanded and they were paid a small wage. After the First World

War the company was a pioneer in what it called 'college apprenticeships'. It took graduates in mechanical and electrical engineering for a two-year training course in manufacturing or design, research or the sales side of engineering. By 1921 its education department was responsible for 1,450 men and boys, including 100 college apprentices, 100 school apprentices and 800 trade apprentices. In 1929 Metro-Vick offered a new scheme, of the sandwich type. The chosen school-leaver had one year's practical training in the works before entering university. He returned to the works during his vacations. After he had completed his university degree, a further year's training at the works completed his apprenticeship. Its apprenticeship schemes leading to professional employment, for graduates and non-graduates, consisted of a series of transfers from one manufacturing department to another to familiarise the apprentice with the manufacturing methods and each department's organisation and problems, but 'Towards the completion of their apprenticeship the apprentices specialize in a particular section of the works, such as manufacturing, design, research, commercial, or accounting, and are given opportunity to enter the departments where they will obtain the necessary experience.'[9] University men who wanted to make a career in works accounting were given preliminary workshop experience, and then transferred to the costing and accounting departments for specialised training. However, while the size of Metro-Vick's training effort was such that the rest of British engineering could be very thankful, too little of it had gone into developing the business capacities of its engineers. The men's fierce pride in Metro-Vick's heavy engineering skills was matched only by their distaste (widespread amongst technical men) for the book-keepers. 'We used to regard accountants as servants and inferiors', confirmed one of them some years later.[10]

In firms where the production function or engineering considerations dominated, the technical men with no knowledge of marketing and no interest in finance could have a profound effect on performance. They influenced decision-making either from their strong position as technical men or as senior managers, which they had reached because they were seen as the most necessary people in the firm, not because they exhibited a high level of managerial competence. In Standard Telephones and Cables, which was a company with an organisational split between manufacturing on the one side and engineering and sales on the other, the engineers (some of whom were graduates) took the most senior positions. They had few business skills, and as late as the mid-1950s making a profit came fairly low on their list of priorities. Orders came when STC engineers discussed with customers' engineers what was required: the all-important thing was to produce a product to satisfy both sets of engineers. Money management was of the most rudimentary kind. There was no promotion from outside, which might have brought in stronger business skills and new ideas. The historian of the company has noted that, in the 1950s,

In the closed world of STC there was no management training. One man went to the Harvard Business School but he was an exception and he came back confused. People were promoted who were not fully competent or trained for the job and they had to learn as they went along. There were not enough people of the right calibre to deal with the problems the company had. In the middle of the decade it had been slow to respond to new competitor challenges in export markets yet it was diversifying into things like computers without having the talents to understand the different businesses, evaluate projects and control expenditures. At the same time the company was not investing enough in its machines. Crowded workshops were in need of modernisation. Above all, a completely new attitude, nothing less than a cultural change, was needed to running a business in the latter half of the twentieth century.[11]

The 'flaccid' organisation was being run by 'an ageing group of inbred engineers', with almost disastrous consequences for the company in the post-1945 world.

The feature of 'inbred engineers' in management was widespread. Both the electricity supply and gas supply industries were too much dominated by engineers with little experience or interest outside of engineering. In the 1920s, both industries were composed of mostly small undertakings all making their own technical decisions, little influenced by commercial considerations, and the need for standardisation. In 1926 a report on electricity supply found, amongst other things, that a restriction to expansion 'arises from a tendency prevalent in this country to regard the engineering side as necessarily being of higher status and greater importance than the commercial side'.[12] Government intervention pushed electricity generation into some reform in the late 1920s. It set up the Central Electricity Board (with a commercial remit) for wholesaling electricity, which produced the national grid. By the late 1930s electricity generation was close, if not quite equal to, its foreign counterparts, while the grid was a method of distributing electric power which had no equal in the world.[13] But the retail sales end had been left in the hands of the undertakings, and the engineers. Thus 'many of the industry's senior men clearly still accorded pride of place to engineering, with the emphasis on hardware and its technical efficiency rather than on financial and sales questions and service to the consumer', a characteristic which was damaging to the industry's prospects.[14] The gas industry, although much regulated, had had less constructive government intervention, and gas entered the Second World War growing, but at a decreasing rate, and with no real strategy to meet the increasing competition from electricity. A report on gas in 1939 painted a picture of an industry needing radical improvement if it were going to compete. Despite all its technical difficulties, substantial improvements had been within its grasp. There was a great need, the authors of the report advised, for higher standards of personnel at the top levels. For important technical and administrative posts, 'more attention should be paid nationally to the sources of good material. There are many methods of recruitment by establishment of grants and scholarships and co-operation with educational authorities. Above all, the prestige of the industry must be high and the prospects attractive if results are to be obtained.'[15] The dominance of the unbusinesslike engineers had been a significant drawback to the industry's progress. The report concluded that 'there has been, and still is, considerable apathy in large sections of the industry regarding marketing efficiency. This is to some extent due to the tradition of the gas industry that the engineer plays a dominating part in the management.'[16] The industry had recognised it needed to meet the competition from electricity, and endeavoured to counter it with improved service, salesmanship and publicity, but what it had managed to do was too little and too patchy.

One of the better efforts for the gas industry had been made by the Gas Light and Coke Company, which by the 1930s employed about 20,000 of the industry's 230,000 employees (the British gas industry was the largest in Europe). The company was amongst the most progressive on the technical side and, with the establishment in 1926 of an adequately equipped laboratory for research, it had an infusion of young scientists from Oxford.[17] In the late 1920s its energetic Controller of Gas Sales, Francis Goodenough, began experimenting with sales apprenticeships for school-leavers from the private schools. Over a four-year period these staff pupils attended evening classes to acquire the National Certificate for Gas Supply, and were put through a programme of planned experience. 'They entered the offices, the workshops, for the technical side of the business, the laboratories, and one branch of the Sales Department after another until at the end of the four years they were competent to act as assistant representatives.'[18] The company also began to give assistance to 'promising members of the clerical staff who wish to take such examinations as that for the B.Com. of the London University, or those of the Chartered Institute of Secretaries, and similar bodies'. But after Goodenough, a 'born publicist', left in the early 1930s, his successor was the Distributing Engineer.[19] In 1935 the company took a formal decision to attempt no further expansion by amalgamation, acknowledging that any larger unit would be unmanageable without major organisational change.[20] The image of the gas industry after 1945 was still 'honest but old-fashioned, dull and dirty'.[21] The roles of the gas engineer and manager remained intertwined.

It was not only electricity *supply* which was dominated and held back by technical men interested primarily in the technical aspects of their firms' products. The important electrical *manufacturing* was also hit. The early profits in the industry had come from the manufacture of the humble lamp, but when companies moved into heavy electricals their interest was captured by heavy engineering to an unhealthy extent. There were three principal groupings of electrical manufacturers in the 1920s, GEC, English Electric, and AEI, and between them they enjoyed up to 60 per cent of the market on the heavy plant side. In the late 1920s, the new range of goods, like radios, batteries, lamps, valves, refrigerators and vacuum cleaners flooded into the home market, mainly from America.[22] The imposition of higher tariffs gave British firms a much needed breathing space, and some took it, although the subsidiaries of foreign firms, such as Hoover and Electrolux, did better than most. Yet the large firms in the industry continued to be preoccupied with heavy electrical plant, to an extent which damaged their appliance firms' ability to compete. AEI's company secretary openly admitted in 1954 that its domestic appliance business had been performing badly for years through neglect. Its poor performance, 'was not the fault of the men who worked for

Hotpoint; we had always regarded ourselves as a heavy engineering company, and what money there was for capital development had gone into the heavy side of the business, to the starvation of the appliance side'.[23] The heavy section had operated in a different business world. The industry, like so many others in the inter-war years, 'had been dominated by an international cartel or ring of companies who carved up markets between themselves, shared technical information, fixed prices and discouraged new competitors from entering the industry'.[24] The industry had been sufficiently shielded from market forces to allow the three big electrical companies to become dominated by engineers 'who were primarily dedicated to producing the heavy electrical plant for power stations. They produced a fine product, sometimes regardless of cost … . The heavy electrical men were production-orientated like much of British industry. Marketing and financial control in the American sense were unknown to them.' The final reckoning came in the 1960s, when 'all three companies faced a serious decline in profitability and experienced a loss of confidence in their ability to manage themselves'.[25] GEC was fortunate to have had Hugo Hirst – a salesman with an eye for a main chance – at its head for many years, but even this had not saved it for the longer term. A figures man with business skills, Arnold Weinstock, showed the engineers how it was done.

Even the progressive Imperial Chemical Industries had allowed technical men, with almost no wider business understanding, to move into high administrative positions in the divisions. Nobel Industries, one of the four constituent companies of the merger which produced ICI, had brought into the new combine the practice of recruiting very able scientists and engineers for the technical side and bright schoolboys for the non-technical, both sides normally keeping to their own domain. 'The general underlying idea was that there were two kinds of staff, technical and commercial, and that the training of each unfits him for the work of the other.'[26] However, when the reorganisation of ICI took place just after the merger, it was found impossible to fill the new administrative positions without calling on the technical staff. Some of these became very capable executives, but the shortage had brought home to Head Office the need to ensure that sufficient supplies of good men were available in the future.

ICI, along with a number of other manufacturing firms in the late 1920s, recognised and began trying to tackle the problem of management succession. The merger wave, the expansion of manufacturing output, the increasing specialisation of tasks, the attempts at rationalisation, and the gap left by the 'lost generation' of the First World War, had all begun to contribute to a paucity of good men in industry from the late 1920s. Some firms, like parts of Standard Telephones and Cables, chose not to expand further and so reduce their need for managerial expertise. But some decided that they would make special efforts to produce a small number of high-quality people rather than rely on the market or the normal promotional practices to produce them. Training schemes to produce high-level managers was not a new idea. The Calico Printers Association were being advised of the benefits to the enterprise of such practices as early as 1902. 'The most successful branches should become training schemes for such men', wrote a CPA director, 'from which they can be drafted to positions of responsibility, facilitating the introduction of the best methods of the leading houses into the less successful branches.'[27] But the idea of a 'management trainee scheme' became quite fashionable in the 1930s amongst very large firms. After the Second World War there was a marked expansion of this type of scheme. The apprenticeship system, based on learning whilst earning, was very well known and understood as a means of training young people, and the management trainee schemes were based on similar principles, but to produce junior executives rather than skilled craftsmen. Like apprenticeship, management trainee schemes were usually of a pre-determined length of time; the trainees relied on the existing experienced men to teach them; there was much menial work in the early months; and there was no certainty of the men being taken on by the firm at the end of the time. It will be seen from the examples below that while the firms which took on management trainees were amongst the UK's largest employers and with a good reputation for training, the schemes, and in particular the main element of planned experience, were with one exception, very restrained efforts.

While ICI's efforts were more successful than most, and Head Office attached great importance to the quality of the company's top staff, its response to the problem of providing the new men capable of leading this giant new enterprise was much less than vigorous. Soon after the formation of ICI in 1926, Head Office saw a need to raise the general level of ability throughout the organisation, and more especially to provide ICI with a number of outstanding men for the future. It began very sensibly by attempting to get for ICI supplies of the most able young people leaving education. It thought that they would be found in the most expensive public schools. 'It is quite clear', wrote the company secretary (an old Etonian),

that, at the present moment, our men however good they may be, are too much on the same plane. We have a few men who may go far in the future but in view of the numbers we employ the proportion of men of any personality is relatively small and I believe that the proportion will be largely increased if we get the best type of public school boy, realising as we do, that work alone is not the only necessary qualification for success.[28]

It set up links with a number of schools, with the aims of encouraging the study of science and attracting boys to a career in ICI. It agreed to interview interested boys and those who passed the interview, and then took a degree from Oxford or Cambridge, would be guaranteed a place in the company. The scheme got off to a bad start as not enough suitable boys came forward. It was re-vamped in 1930. The schoolboys now chosen for the technical side were required to get their degree from Oxford or Cambridge and then complete one year's research – after which a job in ICI would be theirs. Those on the commercial side had to complete an Oxbridge degree of any kind and then to read economics, foreign languages, or attend a business school for one year. Only a small number of young men had gone through the scheme before it was ended. The company still thought that not enough of the best pupils were coming forward. But more importantly, the company's commitment made to the schoolboys was proving burdensome. The company had to have suitable posts ready at the right time for boys whom it might no longer consider suitable. But there was the added disadvantage that it was no longer free to choose men who now impressed them more. The scheme died during the depression.

In 1927 Head Office had begun considering a management trainee scheme, the young men to be Learners for Executive Positions. It decided to set up a central selection committee who would work from a reserve list of possible candidates. The chosen men, six a year, would undergo a two-year training. 'This scheme reached the stage of a printed document, but differences of opinion arose subsequently and it was dropped.'[29]

In 1932 there was much discussion, led by Head Office and involving the University of Cambridge appointments board, on the selection and training of engineers for the senior staff, particularly with a view to giving them 'an opportunity to get some idea of the Company's organisation, processes and technical knowledge before being absorbed on one particular line of work'. But it was not to cost too much. 'Any training scheme adopted inevitably means some deflection of staff from their ordinary work for purposes of instruction and explanation. This should be minimised as far as possible, or training becomes a costly matter.' 'Trainees', it was suggested, 'can actually be given jobs to do or they can be attached to shift managers or sections of the laboratories or plant as supernumaries without much bother.'[30] The cost of training was a major concern at this time. The company had already in 1931 taken the decision *not* to make small grants to junior staff who took university degrees or passed other examinations.[31]

In 1933, Head Office approved a scheme for a central pool of men trained for the higher commercial and administrative posts in the company's service, and from which all vacancies would normally be filled. This, too, was postponed. The groups (or divisions) had firmly resisted the idea of centralisation. Head Office eventually contented itself with trying to ensure that the groups undertook sensible recruitment and training policies for their own men. Thus in the selection and training of managers the groups were very much their own masters.[32] Not until 1937 was there any real advance towards a formal scheme of training. By 1938 thirty commercial trainees (nineteen of them with science degrees) had passed through a two-year course – not a large number for an enterprise employing over 100,000 men in seventy factories in the UK.

In one ICI group at least, new technical staff were getting by 1939 a good introductory training in the form of 'days or weeks in each section of the company (purchasing, accounts, exports, packing, research and various parts of the works) – and some time on particular plants as operatives, chargehands, and foremen'.[33] But group control over training meant that there was little inter-group experience for the men, and the quantity and quality of training varied widely. How much training a man received, and how quickly he was promoted, depended very much on the first department and group he found himself in. Further planned experience after the initial introduction was not common; and there was every indication that the commitment to management development as a whole was pretty low. Head Office was informed in 1937 that for the early training of men,

It is fair to say that no definite system for this purpose exists, but that it is left to the various departments or sections in which a new recruit may find himself to give such training as may be required for the work the recruit has to do. From that point, further training is in most cases haphazard.

In the ICI divisions there was little interest in bringing in graduates and other favoured outsiders onto the non-technical side, and therefore they had a reduced interest in preparing the kind of training programme which would mostly benefit such men. Head Office tried in the early years to press the reluctant divisions to recruit more from the public schools and older universities. Nobel were told that 'it is impossible to conceive that a complete section of the I.C.I. business should be in such a condition that it is impossible to introduce University men into it'.[34] Some educational grants were given, but 'the total educational budget for 1937 ... amounted to only £1,576 which gives a measure of the total effort in this direction. This expenditure related to the Groups only and nothing is spent in respect of the staff at Headquarters.'[35] It was suggested in 1939 that they were still training specialists rather than all-round men, and that potential managers were too restricted in their activities.

After the Second World War an internal judgement on previous efforts in ICI was not flattering: 'The inability of certain Divisions to fill "high level" vacancies in their Divisions and the general shortage of staff in I.C.I. suitable for such vacancies is a serious condition which has arisen from two main causes (a) faulty selection of staff and inadequate forward planning, and (b) failure properly to train, develop and use staff.'[36] ICI began to recruit engineers and arts graduates centrally, with the idea of making able men, now difficult to come by in sufficient numbers, widely available in the company. But the training provision for new men remained haphazard, as were the chances of gaining wider experi-

ence for the route upwards. One arts graduate who joined Dyestuffs Division in 1949 recalled that 'Although it had become a
policy of ICI centrally to recruit arts graduates, the Board of
Dyestuffs Division did not at first have the faintest idea how to
train me or use me. I wasted eighteen months on a training course
that could easily have been completed in a quarter of that time.'[37]
This arts graduate began to take an interest in politics and

was then summoned by senior management and told that as the Company could no longer be sure where my real interests lay, in ICI or in
politics, a tour of duty abroad which was being laid on for me exceptionally at that stage of my ICI career was being cancelled ... . Evidently
I had been selected as a 'high-flyer' and I had thrown it all away.

The divisions had developed along different lines, each with its
own characteristics and personality, and management development
was treated very differently in each. But what had remained
characteristic of them all was the low level of interest in the
commercial aspects of business. The enterprise had been very
much biased towards the technical rather than the commercial side
of affairs from its inception. 'The commercial side, generally
speaking, was not held in high esteem and the difference between
the way technical staff, on the one hand, and commercial staff, on
the other, were selected made it certain that the ablest men would
usually be found on the technical side.'[38] The low level of commercial expertise led to some very expensive mistakes, but still
after the Second World War and the break up of the pre-war
cartels and agreements, ICI was very much technical rather than
commercial in orientation. The engineers ruled Billingham and the
scientists ruled the Winnington plant, and both looked down on
the commercial needs of the business. The new chairman in 1953
(a chemist) was, like his much of his Board, 'commercially
naïve'.[39] ICI encountered 'substantial managerial difficulties in
coping with both the rate of technological change and heightened
international competition that they and others faced from about
the mid-1950s onwards'.[40] The easy times were over for ICI: their
efforts to train up men had been more influenced by personal
preferences than the necessity of preparing the company for the
future.

The United Steel Companies was unusual in deciding that it
needed new men with wider capabilities at the same time that it

was undergoing centralisation. The British steel industry had been in the doldrums in the 1920s, but by 1927 the outlook seemed more promising and United Steel decided to make radical changes. It had been a loosely structured combine from its registration in 1918, and better control demanded stronger centralisation before it could begin to consider the more modern version of industrial structure – decentralisation into divisions or groups.

United Steel embarked on centralisation with a will, and set up schemes of training for the men it would need – these were to be primarily university graduates and public schoolboys. There were two programmes (of two years) on offer, one for the technical side, one for the marketing. 'An important part of the training would be the provision of experience at each of the various branches of the Company.'[41] After one year there were over twenty men in training. In the early 1930s the company took twelve graduates at a time for the two-year course and as many trainees direct from schools. The University of Cambridge appointments board thought that United Steel had one great virtue – they did not sack people but managed to find them a job somewhere in the organisation. The new men, however, suffered not least from the drawback of being part of a very centralised organisation. They had little chance to develop or use their managerial abilities. The company had a noticeable gap in the middle levels of central management. The two years of practical training became more valuable to both technical and marketing men after the war when United Steel began to decentralise its organisation. However, long before this time it had become clear that the British steel industry was a failing industry. The new men could have no measurable effect on the underlying problems facing steel in the short or medium term.

Some of those more enterprising firms in the 1920s attempting management trainee schemes had earlier tried to produce their new managers from school-leavers rather than graduates. Tootal Broadhurst and Lee's schemes had produced mill managers on the technical side (see p. 127 above), and departmental managers on the other (the other being 'merchanting'). Its training for 'merchanting' (buying and selling, as distinct from works management) offered apprentices in the 1920s 'periods of training in the counting house, shipping office, and representative departments, up to the age of twenty-one, and are eligible for some experience in the Continental branch'.[42] At the end of the apprenticeship they 'may be placed on the regular staff and promoted according to ability and opportunity to positions of increasing responsibility in direct contact with buyers and salesmen'. However, whatever expectations the company had of this merchanting scheme, they were not met, and it was dropped. The system of moving apprentices automatically from department to department was discarded, for the reason that 'entrants do not feel the urge to work their way up, and they do not appreciate the value of small economies and of competitive effort'.[43] The company took on school and university apprentices in the 1930s, but now the apprentices were shown the work of one department and then made to wait for promotion before they were moved. 'Training is not given as a progressive experience automatically, but is obtained as service and by promotion on ability.'[44] Whether the change was intended to help remedy the situation or merely to penalise the later recruits was not made clear. Neither type of scheme, however, was able to produce the type of man that was sought for the top positions in the firm from the late 1920s, and the directors began to look to Cambridge University for more promising material. They offered a one-year training scheme and evening classes paid for by the company. But the Second World War had begun before this new scheme had proved its worth.

The name of Rowntree was equated with good working conditions and exceptional educational facilities for its young employees. Seebohm Rowntree's interest in scientific management led him to promote education for all levels of management in British industry, and graduates were being brought into his firm in the mid-1920s with the very top positions open to them. Rowntrees, however, got itself into financial difficulties; the old directors took a back seat and an accountant, George Harris, who had married into the family, took charge. The company was turned around in the 1930s, and a trainee scheme set up 'to provide for the firm's future requirements in the way of trained and capable executive officers'.[45] It looked very good on paper. For three years young men, chosen both from the staff and from outside, were to be given a thorough grounding of one of the main branches of the business, spending some time working in the factory, sitting in at committee meetings, and filling temporary vacancies. More broadly, trainees were to be given 'a knowledge of the Company's policy and practice by means of courses of lectures on these and related topics, and regular meetings of the trainee staff, at which business conditions are reviewed and matters of current trade interest are discussed'.[46] The University of Cambridge appointments board which were asked to supply men to Rowntree were, however, less than impressed by Rowntree's efforts. According to the board it was they who had in 1932 'pressed hard for some sort of training scheme for the regular recruitment of such men' and the company promised to consider it – 'but object on the score of expense'.[47] In 1934 the board noted that there was 'something in the nature of a trainee scheme' which was not getting the best of material through it.[48] It would appear that there was some gap in the 1930s between what this company, and others, wanted and what it was able and prepared to invest to get it.

One of the railway companies, the LNER, had got off to an effective and very early start in efforts to infuse the management with younger yet experienced men. In the 1890s the new General Manager of the NER, as part of the radical reforms he was instituting, began hand-picking graduates and others for early responsibility and wide experience before their first senior appointment. These young men were termed Traffic Apprentices, but other bright employees were also picked out for early responsibility.[49] From this time the NER (in 1923 the LNER) put great efforts into the education of its employees. The Traffic Apprenticeships continued throughout the inter-war period, but, along with the railways themselves after the Railway Act of 1921, they became gradually much less vigorous and more bureaucratic. By the late 1930s there were two sets of apprentices, twenty-five in each, for three years' training. The programme of training now covered 'short spells respectively at small country stations, large parcels and goods offices, yard-masters' offices, dock offices, engine sheds, district passenger, goods, operating, and locomotive running offices ... as well as some time in Head Offices'.[50] The company still went to the universities, particularly Cambridge, for men, but LNER salaries were far lower than those of the other main-line railways and it was not a first choice for a career. The training scheme did not invigorate men with the idea that the LNER was looking for and was receptive to new ideas. The new recruits, however able, became part of the general in-breeding. 'On the way up, especially in the inter-war years, men were plentiful but equipment was old and scarce. Hence the fetish, once in power for solving yesterday's problems.'[51] Quite a number left the railway to find a successful career in business. But the LNER had done more than most to produce railway managers and there was a predominance of former LNER traffic apprentices in BR in the early years after nationalisation.[52]

Overall, whilst the management trainee schemes promoted the companies to the outside world, they did not go far towards producing the men for the future. Their methods had been fairly limited, many involved not much more than a 'Cook's tour' of the various departments of the company, relying heavily on the interest and ability of the senior men to provide the training, with no extra support. The numbers receiving the training were very small. Few firms had taken up the idea in any systematic way before the Second World War. Less than twenty firms can be identified as having attempted a formal scheme with a regular intake. Others took one or two men as trainees on an irregular basis. In a survey in the late 1930s, of 114 firms taking Cambridge graduates in 1937–38, only twelve had training schemes. Twenty-two graduates out of 326 in the survey referred to their firms as having one.[53] Many firms had encountered difficulties with their schemes which they had not been able, and sometimes not prepared, to overcome.

The initial selection of men who would do well was always a great problem whether they were being put on a scheme or not. Firms generally were not very good at picking out potential businessmen, particularly from amongst a batch of university graduates, usually Cambridge arts graduates. Unilever was one company prepared to admit 'faulty judgement' on its part. Some firms knew that they were looking for men of 'the public school type', but whether they thought they had found them or no, the results were often disappointing. Cambridge was informed in 1939 that 'Sir Andrew Agnew of the Shell has stated publicly that the Shell have never had one Cambridge man from the Appointments Board who has really been an outstanding success.'[54] Shell's Administrative Cadet scheme was dropped. In Tootal, Broadhurst and Lee at one period only one in four taken for the commercial side did any good.[55] But firms recruited so few men to each trainee scheme that the choice had to be good for the scheme to have any value. A large recruiter like Unilever was taking only around eight potential managers a year by the late 1930s. Not all firms recruited regularly, which would have given them more experience at choosing men. This was for the good reason that not all firms were yet attempting to forecast their future managerial requirements and how many new recruits would be needed to meet them. Cadbury Brothers was still unusual in the 1930s in wanting to forecast the requirements of likely men for specific departments for some years ahead. This became a more usual exercise after the Second World War with the increase in personnel managers.

The companies had also chosen to restrict their choice of graduate recruit primarily to men from the universities of Oxford and Cambridge. Not only did they expect to find the right type of man there, but they looked there first as a matter of course. The long tradition in the middle classes of equating 'the universities' with only the two older universities was very strong amongst middle-class businessmen. The practice was also widespread amongst Oxbridge alumni of giving first refusal of any position they had at their disposal to men from their own university. Thus the management trainees in all the known schemes were more likely than not to be Oxbridge graduates. A 1950s survey of sixty-eight management trainees found that they were preponderantly arts graduates from Oxford or Cambridge, and that there were seldom young staff on management trainee schemes.[56] Restricting the sources unnecessarily restricted the selection.

Once they had their men, the firms were confronted with the dilemma of how to convert them into managers. They accepted that learning under instruction was the best approach, but nothing much was done to prepare and persuade existing managers that this extra task should be given a high priority. And while the trainees were men who would soon be needed in senior management, how was the firm to get the best of them to the top? Should the trainees be treated as an elite in order to close the management gap quickly? They were special, but not very special. They had potential, but no skills. They were wanted at the top, but only if they could prove they deserved to be there. The general response was to consider the initial induction course to be sufficient interference by management with the natural forces which would propel good men upwards. In these firms, the men joined the normal promotional practices after the introduction was over, whatever those normal practices were. Where these allowed a favoured man to move up quickly the graduate trainee might be so favoured, but otherwise the man joined a department in a junior capacity, and worked his way up through the ranks. This usually put him in a more favoured position than those starting at the very bottom, but it also had the effect of putting him on the first rung of a specialist career, rather than the first step towards management. Employees of British firms had normally to acquire specialist skills and move upwards inside a function. Without planned opportunities for wider experience after the initial introductory course, the men could at best become functional specialists with a somewhat wider knowledge of the company than was usual.

Finally, the commitment to the success of the schemes was not very strong. Where they were seen not to be working very well or causing too many problems, they were more likely to be phased out than re-worked. Only a few firms, like Harrods and Unilever, were prepared to try again and again to get a good scheme in place. Unilever, a marketing-orientated firm, is one company which gave high priority to producing able men in the inter-war period, using trainee schemes and planned experience to good effect. It had been formed in 1929, as a holding company with a controlling interest in the Lever group of companies in the UK and the Dutch Margarine Union. The merger had been a defensive move – a response to the increasing competition in static markets for soap and margarine and the continuing threats to basic raw material supplies – but the resulting conglomerate did not adopt timid policies. Its constituent company heads accepted that they were going to be part of a whole, and Unilever was going to achieve this with the help of the Unilever managers. Unilever's 'directors and experts from the controlling committees of both Dutch and English companies travelled endlessly, reporting on factories, politics, economic trends, and, most important, on men. For given the right man in the right job there was not much to worry about.'[57]

Each operating company handled its own recruiting and training at all levels, except the most senior. They all relied heavily on recruiting the brightest boys leaving the local schools and giving them a comprehensive training in-house, in line with the parent company's policy. This provided the main body of management plus a large proportion of senior management. The parent company itself controlled the appointment of the most senior posts. To have sufficient numbers of good men available Unilever also ran a centrally-controlled management trainee scheme.

The chairman, although he was not a university graduate, joined the committee of the Cambridge University appointments board, and decided that the scheme would cater for about six men a year, primarily from Oxford and Cambridge. Occasionally it included an existing member of the staff of approximately the same age. The training was done in the operating companies. It became the responsibility of the top man in a Unilever company, not the under-managers who may or may not have had the ability, time, or interest in helping young men to become better managers than *they* were, and the programme was a comprehensive one. Lever Bros had begun a new scheme in 1928.

The scheme is to put one man to each of various associated companies, as protégé of the Chairman, who is thenceforward his boss and should train him and watch him carefully, perhaps calling for an essay every three months on what he has learnt. Ordinarily the first year would be in a factory in England; the second year abroad, the Continent or say Canada; the third, at least in part, in London: thus showing them in order production, distribution, and selling, with the central administration to cap all.[58]

They had set up an appointments committee to guard against too many men with influence gaining a place. All trainees were expected to be fluent in German before they went abroad. The three years were considered a probation, but the trainees were paid 'an adequate allowance'. If they proved suitable they joined the permanent staff of a company in a junior managerial capacity 'whether at the moment we have a definite job for him or not. If there is not actually a vacancy at the time, one is pretty sure to arise.'[59]

There was always a very large number of applicants for each place on the scheme, and the appointments boards filtered the men through the early stages. The company attached no importance to the subject read at university. Despite all this, however, there were problems with the early intakes. The company admitted it had had problems 'due partly no doubt to faulty judgment on our part, and partly to the fact that the Universities did not understand our requirements', but from the early 1930s they had very good results and the failures before the Second World War were the exception rather than the rule.[60] The judgement of one of the trainees in

1939 was that 'one is given every chance of learning as much as one can'.[61]

Up to 1939, the scheme seemed to be working well, and it was restarted after the war. But the scale was now too small, and it was felt that the operating companies needed to use graduates much more. It was also admitted of the trainee scheme that it was geared to the small number of very top posts, to the neglect of the lower levels: 'what we were really trying to do was to select a few potential Directors – we were not doing this intentionally but it was the inevitable consequence'.[62] Unilever also realised that the very small numbers being recruited led to a loss of interest by the appointments boards. It also realised that it was rejecting large numbers of other very able men who might have been of great value to the company.

From the late 1940s, Unilever Head Office extended its contacts with the universities and recruited graduates in much larger numbers: it put these approved candidates forward for the operating companies to make their selection. The Unilever Companies Management Development Scheme was established in 1952. This used the latest techniques to help reduce the mistakes on selection (the intake had risen to around 100 a year in the UK and another 100 on the Continent by the 1960s). The trainees were put through various courses to enlarge their understanding of the business and then moved into on-the-job training.[63] The successful men were added to a list of potential managers, and their progress and placements were watched by a committee of managers. Potential top managers were not assumed to need no more planned experience once they had proved themselves capable. Rather, they were moved sideways and upwards to a remarkable extent throughout the Unilever empire.

The benefits of all this were considerable to Unilever and not just to the men being trained. Unilever was a multinational corporation and the associated companies needed the stimulus of new men as much as the new men needed the stimulus of a challenge. Despite the strength of identity felt by many of Unilever's associated companies – Bird's Eye, Walls, Lever Brothers, Van den Berghs, Batchelors – the senior managers in them became on the whole Unilever and not company men. Their loyalties lay with the management which controlled their careers. Movement had also counteracted much of the danger of patches of stagnation. Most importantly, it produced for Unilever managers of a calibre and in numbers which could not have been produced either by the external labour market or the internal promotional practices characteristic of much of the rest of British industry.

The size, structure, and product of a firm could be inappropriate for much movement of young executives, and the departments might resist continually giving experience to young men who were destined to be with them only a short while, but most large companies in the UK had the capacity to bring planned experience more into use. Inter-company training, which a small number of firms of all sizes used without great difficulty, could have been used on a wider scale. The obvious dangers of specialisation could have been met rather better by periods of external training and more opportunities for staff at all levels to meet. One of the good points mentioned by trainees of their induction courses was the contacts they made (amongst their peers as well as their seniors) and which greatly helped to break down barriers.

The harder manpower market after the Second World War and the expansion of business activity, along with the availability of rather more cash for peripheral activities, encouraged firms to make more use of planned experience than they had done previously. Management trainee schemes, which were known to attract better recruits, became more widespread. Large firms began to set up their own residential training centres. But still in the mid-1950s, management training was still very underdeveloped. A study in 1956 of fifty-one large companies found that one-third had no organised system of management training, and perhaps one in ten used internal job rotation.[64] A decade later, it was estimated that four out of five large companies had no systematic training scheme.[65]

At the beginning of the 1960s, of the 11,000 public companies and 310,000 private companies, around 400 gave its managers some management training.[66] And of the half million managers in industry, less than one per cent had received any form of external management training. It was judged that 'for the majority of managers in British industry the provision of the proper opportunities is still a matter of "the luck of the draw" rather than the result of a management development programme'.[67] British industry by the onset of the 1960s had rejected the help of the education system in producing men partly prepared for business management, arguing that it preferred the time to be spent on-the-job. But it then also rejected the opportunity for experience-based learning which time spent on-the-job offered.

References

1 *Britain's Industrial Future*, Report of the Liberal Industrial Inquiry, Ernest Benn Ltd, 1928, p. 131.

2 University of Cambridge Appointments Board (UCAB), Graduates' Replies, 8 January 1939, ref: APTB 14/14.

3 P. Young, *Power of Speech: A History of Standard Telephones and Cables 1883–1983*, George Allen and Unwin, 1983, p. 137.

4 ICI memorandum, 'The recruitment, training and promotion of technical staff', 2 March 1948, p. 5, File: Staff recruitment and training, Box 274.

5 R. W. Ferguson, ed., *Training in Industry*, Pitman, 1935, p. 8.

6 B. Monck, 'The eclipse of the engineer in management', *Engineering*, 10 September 1954, p. 330.

7 Monck, 'The eclipse', p. 329.

8 Association for Education in Industry and Commerce (AEIC), *Report on Education for Management*, AEIC, May 1928 ed., p. 24.

9 Ferguson, *Training*, p. 112.

10 R. Jones and O. Marriott, *Anatomy of a Merger: A History of G.E.C., A.E.I., and English Electric*, Jonathan Cape, 1970, p. 153.

11 Young, *Power of Speech*, p. 138.

12 In Political and Economic Planning (PEP), *Report on the Gas Industry in Great Britain*, PEP, March 1939, p. 142.

13 S. Pollard, *The Development of the British Economy 1914–1967*, Edward Arnold, 1969 ed., p. 99.

14 L. Hannah, *Electricity before Nationalisation: A Study of the Development of the Electricity Supply Industry in Britain to 1948*, Macmillan, 1979, p. 152.

15 PEP, *Report on the Gas Industry in Great Britain*, March 1939, p. 26.

16 PEP, *Report on the Gas Industry*, p. 142.

17 T. I. Williams, *A History of the British Gas Industry*, Oxford University Press, Oxford, 1981, p. 72.

18 F. Goodenough, address to the Selling Section of the Management Research Groups, Minute 31 May 1929, MRG Box 14.

19 S. Everard, *The History of the Gas Light and Coke Company, 1812–1949*, Ernest Benn, 1949, p. 321.

20 Williams, *A History of the British Gas Industry*, p. 73.

21 F. A. Burden, pamphlet, 'Watson House, 1926–1976, Bulletin Jubilee Supplement', Watson House, 1976, p. 67.

22 T. May, *An Economic and Social History of Britain 1760–1970*, Longman, 1987, p. 335.

23 In R. S. Edwards and H. Townsend, *Business Enterprise: Its Growth and Organisation*, Macmillan, 1958, p. 312.

24 Jones and Marriott, *Anatomy*, p. 13.

25 Jones and Marriott, *Anatomy* p. 13.

26 ICI, Memorandum from G. P. Pollitt, 27 June 1933, p. 2, File: Staff recruitment and training, Box 274.

27 H. W. Macrosty, *The Trust Movement in British Industry*, Longman, 1907, p. 384.

28 ICI, Letter from P. C. Dickens, 3 March 1927, File CR/215/7, Box 457.

29 ICI, Note by W. H. Coates, 'The training of personnel', September 1937.

30 ICI, Letter from F. Spickernell on 'Engineers training scheme', 8 June 1933, ref. CACM 674.

31 ICI Minute 280, 28 September 1931, ref. CAC, Box 274.

32 W. J. Reader, *Imperial Chemical Industries: A History: The First Quarter-Century 1926–1952*, II, Oxford University Press, Oxford, 1975, p. 73.

33 UCAB, Graduates' Replies, 30 April 1939, APTB 14/14.

34 ICI, Note from Henry Mond, 14 May 1927, File: Public school boys, Box 328.

35 ICI, Memorandum 'The training of personnel', September 1937, p. 7, Box 274.

36 ICI, 'Survey of engineering staff', 4 October 1946, File: Staff recruitment and training, Box 274.

37 E. Dell, 'Business experience', seminar paper, LSE, 14 June 1984.

38 Reader, *Imperial Chemical*, p. 80.

39 G. Turner, *Business in Britain*, Penguin, 1971, p. 147.

40 A. M. Pettigrew, *The Awakening Giant: Continuity and Change in ICI*, Basil Blackwell, Oxford, 1985, p. 58.

41 P. W. S. Andrews and E. Brunner, *Capital Development in Steel*, Basil Blackwood, Oxford, 1951, p. 166.

42 AEIC, *Education for Management*, p. 25.

43 Ferguson, *Training*, p. 95.

44 Ferguson, *Training*, p. 95.

45 Ferguson, *Training*, p. 91.

46 Ferguson, *Training*, p. 91.

47 UCAB, 20 December 1932, Employers' Visits 1932–35, APTB

10/3.

48 UCAB, 13 August 1934, Employers' Visits, APTB 10/3.

49 R. J. Irving, *The North Eastern Railway Company 1870–1914*, Leicester University Press, Leicester, 1976, pp. 214f.

50 Ferguson, *Training*, p. 141.

51 M. R. Bonavia, *Railway Policy between the Wars*, Manchester University Press, Manchester, 1981, p. 35.

52 Bonavia, *Railway Policy*, p. 34.

53 M. Sanderson, *The Universities and British Industry 1850–1970*, Routledge and Kegan Paul, 1972, p. 295.

54 UCAB, memorandum 23 February 1939, APTB 14/3.

55 UCAB, 6 February 1938, Employers' Visits, APTB 10/4.

56 R. V. Clements, *Managers: A Study of their Careers in Industry*, George Allen and Unwin, 1958, p. 38.

57 C. Wilson, *The History of Unilever: A Study in Economic Growth and Social Change*, II, Cassell, 1954, p. 315.

58 UCAB, 2 April 1928, Employers' Visits, APTB 10/2.

59 ICI, Letter from Lever Bros., 4 October 1929, File: Staff recruitment and training, Box 274.

60 UCAB, Letter from Unilever, 9 July 1937, APTB 14/3.

61 UCAB, 27 April 1939, Graduates' Replies, APTB 14/14.

62 A. D. Bonham-Carter, 'What should and can industry do with the graduate recruit when it gets him?', *Report of the Universities and Industry Conference*, October 1952, FBI, p. 39.

63 C. Wilson, *Unilever 1945–1965: Challenge and Response in the Post-War Industrial Revolution*, Cassell, 1968, p. 52.

64 Acton Society Trust, *Management Succession*, AST, 1956, pp. 94–107.

65 PEP, *Attitudes in British Management*, Pelican, 1966, p. 260.

66 N. Fisher, *The Times*, 4 May 1960, p. 19.

67 PEP, *Attitudes*, p. 256.

Chapter 7
Breaking into the uncharmed circle

In 1980, a government committee agreed that 'There is no easy way to break into the circle whereby managers who are not particularly efficient by international standards recruit successors in their own image ... .'[1] It had seemed for a few years in the 1960s that businessmen over a wide range of industries would take the decision themselves to break into that circle in their own firms. Business in the 1960s was faced, on the one hand, with a high level of need for more efficient men. The 1960s had produced an environment markedly more challenging of business skills than previous decades. There were, on the other hand, many influential voices offering to help produce these more efficient men. And management training was becoming fashionable.

Much of this need for better-quality men arose from the increasing level of activity in organisational restructuring, diversification, and mergers, particularly amongst the very largest firms. Surveys of the largest manufacturing companies show that the level of restructuring and diversification activity had been high in the 1950s, and it had increased in the 1960s. In a sample of ninety-two such companies, thirty-one were involved in structural change in the 1950s; they had moved from the functional organisational form to either a holding company or multidivisional structure.[2] In the 1960s, there were as many as forty-six structural changes, thirty-six of which adopted the multidivisional form. The 1960s had been 'marked by the rapid and widespread adoption of the multidivisional organization structure, which superseded other structural forms especially in companies adopting a strategy of widespread or even partial diversification'.[3] The tendency to diversify, into other industries and into foreign markets, had been rapid

150

over both the 1950s and 1960s. The sample showed twenty-nine cases of increased product diversification during the 1950s, and twenty-nine in the 1960s. The proportion in the sample with extensive overseas manufacturing interests had risen from some 29 per cent in 1950 to 58 per cent by 1970. Merger activity had similarly affected a wide range of industries, and it had produced very much larger enterprises.

Merger activity, diversification, and restructuring put greater strain on managerial capacity. So, too, did the more openly competitive environment of the 1960s. The sellers' market of the 1950s had gone. The many and varied restraints to internal and external trade of earlier decades had been dismantled. The major continental economies had completed their phase of post-war recovery, and American firms were moving into the British market. There was, too, the spectre of the European Common Market. British firms had also to contend with the stop-go monetary policy of government, inflation, and continual crises in the field of industrial relations. There was widespread recognition of the burden on management, and an expectation that many more employers would now take steps to raise the level of managerial capacity available to them. Government, employers' associations, individual businessmen, and educationalists all became active in initiatives to persuade them to do so.

Direct intervention by government had begun during the Second World War. Anxiety over the quality of business managers had long preceded the war, but only in 1943 and with the particular interest of Sir Stafford Cripps, had government decided to intervene directly. Then in 1947 it provided the pressure, and the funds, necessary to set up the British Institute of Management as a non-political, non-profit-making, central management organisation. Also in 1947, it accepted the Urwick Committee's proposal for a national professional management qualification. Urwick had been asked to bring some order to the chaos of professional examinations weighing so heavily on the technical colleges, and he had proposed a two-tier qualification. It was hoped that the Intermediate qualification would be accepted by many of the professional institutes as a replacement for their own first stage examinations. The Final examination was to be of two types, one for those aspiring to enter general management, the other for specialists. There were problems with the Urwick scheme as it was finally put into practice, however, and it was not a success. It had attempted to cover too much, and there were criticisms of the quality of the teaching and of the students. By the 1960s it had awarded only 810 certificates and 640 diplomas.[4]

The main focus of attention of all the groups in the 1960s intent on raising managerial standards was on the contribution that education could make, rather than the contribution of in-company training. The most influential concentrated on extending the provision of management education in university-level institutions. 'Management education' was a term used more widely from the early 1960s to indicate a training which overlapped into teaching people how to perform as a member of senior management; 'business education' indicated simply a vocational education for a business career. In 1960, one of these groups established the Foundation for Management Education: this collected sufficient funds from industry to finance a set of teaching experiments at the universities of Bristol, Cambridge and Leeds. The FME extended its patronage to a further nine institutions in 1963, and in the same year the decision was taken to install American-style business schools in the UK. American success in business since the Second World War had been very impressive and the methods and techniques taught in these schools seemed to be making an increasing contribution to American performance. It was not only the British who were impressed with American managers and American business school training, but with its very wide gap in the provision of training for higher-level managerial posts, and the need to provide a route into management for arts graduates, the establishment of expensive postgraduate and post-experience schools for managers seemed particularly appropriate for the UK. Some businessmen saw business schools as offering a means of updating their still young, experienced, middle managers; others saw them, as did the academics, as a means of developing a new breed of young professionals of high academic ability, equipped with the latest management techniques.

The new National Economic Development Council reported in 1963 that Britain had urgent need of at least one high-level new school or institute, on the lines of the top business schools in the US. The Robbins Report recommended that two major postgraduate schools should be built up. Lord Franks, who had been asked to make recommendations, came out in favour of two such schools, one associated with the University of London, the other with the University of Manchester. Government was now persuaded that Britain needed such schools and it agreed to pay half the cost, on a pound for pound basis. The business appeal for funds, sponsored by the BIM, the FBI and the FME, brought in the very large sum of five million pounds by the end of 1964.[5]

The growing interest in business education and management education in the early 1960s prompted a spate of other developments. In 1961, the Urwick Diploma, which was taken at the technical colleges, was converted into the Diploma in Management Studies, as a postgraduate-level qualification. Some colleges offering it co-operated closely with local firms. For example, in the late 1960s there were between 300 and 400 students at St Helens Technical College, 'mainly from Pilkington Brothers Limited who have developed the course with the assistance of the College as part of their management development scheme'.[6] In 1961, too, the Institute of Directors endowed a Fellowship in Management Studies at Oxford. A number of other postgraduate schools were founded just before those at London and Manchester – at Cranfield, Edinburgh, and Imperial College. Other initiatives followed, including in 1965 the Oxford Centre for Management Studies. The new Council for National Academic Awards began to approve the degree courses of the larger technical colleges and polytechnics. Seventeen B.A. courses in business studies (mainly based on economics, sociology, mathematics, accountancy and law) had been approved by the CNAA by 1969. In 1970 it was noted, with approval, that the UK had embarked on a new era of development in management education in the early 1960s, which had accelerated in the second half of the decade, and now looked 'likely to accelerate even more in the next ten years'.[7]

There were by now some thirty-three universities and business schools which offered qualification courses in management and business education. There were 1,780 undergraduate and 1,650 postgraduate students in the university sector, and 2,730 undergraduate and 650 postgraduate students in further education.[8] Further education had also enrolled, in 1969–70, over 18,000 students for the Diploma in Management Studies, the Higher National Diploma and Higher National Certificate qualifications in management and business studies. There were some 13,000–17,000 students on courses leading to the qualifications of the professional institutes in the management field.

There had also been in the 1960s some direct pressure on firms to increase the quantity and quality of the in-company training that they offered. The Industrial Training Act of 1964, which empowered Industrial Training Boards to impose a levy-grant system on employers, covered *all* types of industrial training including the training and development of managers. There was a good deal of opposition to the boards from some parts of industry 'who much disliked the idea of being forced to pay the levy, as well as the obligation imposed on them by the Act of keeping records of expenditure on training and revealing them to outside inspectors'.[9] But by the end of 1969, twenty-eight boards were in operation, and, it has been argued, some were beginning to make an impact on management training. Certainly, more firms were offering training to their managerial work-force. While at the beginning of the decade only about 400 companies in total had been identified as having some kind of management training, a survey in 1970 of nearly 300 organisations revealed that 52 per cent now had management development schemes of some kind.[10] These schemes generally included staff assessment and career planning, as well as on-the-job training and internal and external training courses. Some very large firms, like Pilkingtons, had recently installed comprehensive schemes designed 'to identify, as far as possible, the human assets of the company at all levels and to prepare and operate a plan for the development of potential managers up to their limit'.[11] The larger the firm the more likely it was to have formal arrangements, but some quite small companies, it was reported, had 'excellent schemes and a great deal of formal management training'.[12] While information on the amount of in-company training being undertaken in the late 1960s was difficult to estimate, the bulk of the training was undoubtedly carried out by companies themselves. One study estimated that of the 356,000 people on business courses of all lengths in 1969–70, employers covered 119,000, the independent centres 135,000, further education 81,000, and the university sector 21,000.[13] Eight per cent of all managers in Britain (some 125,000) had attended a course of a week or longer in 1968, and about half of these were external and half internal.[14]

The strength of industry's commitment to raising managerial standards faced a severe challenge with the onset of the economic downturn at the end of the 1960s. In 1971, it was regretted that 'in the present difficult economic situation industry is preoccupied with shorter term considerations – e.g. cost inflation, profit margins and liquidity. In these circumstances, when all forms of expenditure are under pressure, there is naturally some reluctance to invest in activities whose main benefits may be long term and difficult to measure.'[15] There was, too, already much criticism of what was being offered by the education system, at undergraduate, graduate, and post-experience levels. Industry complained that undergraduate courses were not attracting the right type of person needed in business, and their training was not preparing them well enough to be immediately useful to an employer. While the proliferation of short post-experience courses offered a wide choice, there was no easy way for employers to become informed on the real content of courses and their quality. Business found them expensive and the quality very variable. Even before the end of the 1960s employers were attempting to focus their managers' post-experience courses more closely on the needs of the organisation, and there was a strong move towards in-company courses in the larger companies. The postgraduate degree courses attracted the most criticism. Businessmen argued that the men experiencing these long and expensive courses were not of a calibre to justify the expense, and the expectations of the graduates were being raised to an unrealistic level. Business in any case appointed men to general management positions on the strength of their proven capability in business; they were not swayed in their choice by any academic credential awarded by the education sytem. But a more fundamental complaint was that much of what was being taught in the classroom had little relevance to managerial performance.

There was some sympathy for this last complaint amongst management educators themselves. One line of argument was that, as there had been almost no empirical studies of managers at work, that is, no studies of what managers actually do and how they do it, most educators were ill-prepared to help managers do their work more effectively. 'If we do not know what managers do', it was asked, 'how can we claim to teach management to students in business schools?'[16] The little empirical work that had been done pointed to the fact that there was a wide divergence between managerial work as identified by the management theorist, and the work and behaviour of practising managers and

155

executives in business organisations. Whereas the work of all managers, according to the 'classical' school, was concerned with planning, organising, motivating, co-ordinating and controlling, the work of real managers was less tidy, less scientific, and marked more by differences between managers' jobs than by common characteristics.[17] It was seen, firstly, that 'the jobs that executives do are diverse in the extreme, varying according to functional specialism, occupational background, level in the hierarchy, the nature of employing units, the products or services provided, and a very wide range of social and cultural influences'. Secondly, 'executive work is distinguished by its largely unprogrammed character ... . Lack of information is normal, especially "hard" information of a kind potentially relevant to the job.' Thirdly, 'studies employing observation and diary-keeping have shown the pressurised, often-interrupted and predominantly verbal character of executive work'. Moreover, the process of decision-making 'turns out to be far more political, irrational, and lengthy than the advocates of a kind of "scientific" kind of executive work would wish'.[18]

The debate on what the business schools should be offering to managers produced two main strands of response. One pressed for the business schools to identify more closely the markets they could serve best and concentrate on the needs of these markets. The other called for a radical change of approach to the teaching of 'management'. In this camp voices were raised against the adoption by the schools of 'management' as a concept on its own, divorced from the something that is to be managed. This conception of management had been built on certain premises that had long been accepted by management theorists and many businessmen – that there are distinct managerial skills and techniques quite separate from specialist and technical skills; that these managerial skills have universal applicability, and that the higher the managerial post, the more time will be spent on managerial work and the less time on specialist, technical and other non-managerial problems. The business schools saw their task as teaching these distinctly managerial skills and techniques. They did, however, make a distinction between the managerial skills needed by lower-level managers and those needed by top management. The M.B.A. degree aimed to prepare high-level managerial generalists. The two-year M.B.A. has been described as having four common elements:

First to provide a basic 'literacy' in the underlying principles and functions of management. Secondly to give an opportunity to study in greater depth one or more fields such as marketing, production and finance. Thirdly to develop personal abilities, such as problem analysis, decision making and social skills. Fourthly to improve understanding of the totality of a business, its environment and its strategy.[19]

The business schools had, it was observed, 'institutionalized the ideal of "general management" as a distinct set of skills, whose possessors have legitimate authority over technical specialists'.[20] The conception of management as a high-level activity requiring the acquisition of particular knowledge-based skills leant support to the idea that management was a professional activity. The many dangers that professionalisation in British terms would bring with it did not go unnoticed.

Glover led the call for a rejection of the idea of management as a profession, emphasising the inappropriateness of the professional preoccupation with job-holder status, and a static body of knowledge, rather than with performance. It was also pointed out that the successful Germans had not taken this route. Sorge noted that 'It seems to be taken too much for granted that the idea of "management" as a profession is necessarily valuable, that the teaching of general management principles is very useful, and that all those management techniques and structures are superior everywhere.'[21] German managers were expected to have a degree relevant to the technical or commercial side of the enterprise. As they gained promotion they attended courses, which were sometimes in management centres, and they might be taught general management principles, according to the needs of the organisation and the broader needs of the individual. According to Sorge, however, German managers

might find general principles quite stimulating to talk about in the relaxed atmosphere of a centre, away from the rat-race, but they would wonder what use they can make of doctrines like management by objectives, theories X and Y, Harzburger Modell, or something else. They would often find they practise it already, or that their deviation from it is quite justified in view of more individual constraints. It is therefore understandable that managers do not really flock into general management courses.

He concluded that 'it must be highly doubtful whether general management training can be very helpful when it is not superimposed on a layer of better training in a specialism, notably in engineering for manufacturing managers'.[22] This concern for manufacturing was later picked up by Armstrong who criticised a conception of management which 'centred on the direction of enterprise strategy rather than the improvement of productive efficiency at the operational level'.[23] Business schools, it has rightly been seen, while they catered for only very small numbers of students, were helping to confirm the disengagement of British management from the manufacturing process.

But the debate on what could and should be offered to aspiring and practising managers, particularly in the form of postgraduate degree courses, had long lost the interest of the majority of businessmen. Their heightened interest in education and training for their managers had resulted in a marked increase in activity in the 1960s. But it had not been sustained long into the 1970s, when industry had become increasingly preoccupied with economic survival. And business had judged that the new academic management qualifications, like other academic qualifications awarded by the education system, were of limited value when assessing suitability for a management post. The need for a systematic approach to the education and training of managers had become more widely accepted, but the opportunity of the 1960s had not resulted in any fundamental break with tradition.[24] No clear pattern of management formation had yet emerged.

In 1988, Handy identified three main approaches, or tracks, used in British business – the corporate, the academic and the professional. However, the tracks 'are not mutually exclusive, for it is possible to try to combine any two of them, but nor are they easily compatible, for none really accepts the relevance of the others. The result is too often confusion.'[25] None of the three tracks involved as comprehensive a training as those demanded by Britain's competitors.

In the *corporate* approach, British organisations recruited directly from education and provided training and experience geared to a long-term career. The number of such organisations was small, Handy noted, but growing. The corporate approach, more usually adopted by the largest firms, was akin to the Japanese system. British corporations, however, did not give the broad training across functions characteristic of Japanese firms: the great bulk of early training and experience was confined to one function only. The Japanese also trained more thoroughly and over a longer period than was normal in British firms. For example, on-the-job training in Japanese companies 'is a sequence of specific tasks, projects and targetted performances built around the job, these are reviewed with mentors, analysed in essays, discussed with supervisors and supplemented with "self-enlightenment" (private study from correspondence courses or recommended texts) and by classroom study in formal internal courses'. Such training was used not only in the early years, but even for the training and development of top management.[26] Commitment by the individual to their own development was expected to be as high as the commitment of the company.

The *academic* approach in British firms, as in American, looked to the education system to provide would-be managers with a business education. As in America, there was an increasing demand from students for business courses of all kinds, and, as in America, it was not easy for students to find their way through the jungle of courses, many of uncertain value. But, unlike America, most managers in Britain 'have not themselves experienced any part of the academic approach since leaving school and do not therefore have a very good understanding of it or sympathy for it'. In the US, formal business qualifications were widespread amongst managers, and this formed only one part of their development not the whole.

Lastly, there was the *professional* approach – the acquisition of a professional qualification. This well-trodden route to management allowed students to earn while they learned. British managers with professional qualifications were, like German managers, essentially functional specialists who had taken on extra responsibilities. But while German managers had experienced a higher, relevant education, providing them with a good foundation for specialist training and for general management training later in their career, the examinations of the British professional bodies were narrowly focused on a specialism. 'Accountants, for instance, are trained to be accountants, not businessmen or managers.'[27]

The effort put into this wide variety of approaches in Britain had not yet provided for the nation a well-educated and trained industrial management. A survey by the DTI in 1985[28] of over 2,000 firms revealed, firstly, that 56.1 per cent offered *no* formal management training, relying on men to learn and improve through practice alone. In this 56.1 per cent not one manager undertook a single short internal or external course. Twenty per cent of the large companies (employing over 1,000 employees) did not reach this minimum standard. It was estimated that UK managers received an average of about one day's formal training a year: the majority of managers received none. Companies in food, drink, tobacco and chemical manufacturing – industries which have been notably good performers since the late nineteenth century – showed a greater propensity to train. Thirty-five per cent of the non-trainers had commented that no training was necessary: their managers' existing skills were sufficient. In the same year, 1985, the Labour Force Survey of educational qualifications showed that 12.1 per cent of the 2.5 million male managers in Britain had a degree, 6.2 per cent had attained membership of a professional institution, and 5.6 per cent an HNC/HND. Of the total, 19.1 per cent had no qualification of any kind.[29] Top managers were rather better educated – 24 per cent had a degree.

The renewed interest in management education and training from the late 1980s has led inevitably to calls for a greater provision of courses to be made available in the education system, for new qualifications to be established and for changes to be made to existing offerings to accord more with the needs of industry. Handy's team called for a new professional qualification. Part One would cover business education and would be recommended to all other relevant professional bodies, and to employers outside industry. Part Two would cover management development, in a form which combined study and practice, and which sought to test competence as well as knowledge.[30] The new Management Charter Initiative (an employer-led organisation designed to promote more effective management) followed this with attempts to produce 'competence standards', where managerial competences were defined as 'the knowledge, skills and qualities required of effective managers/leaders'.[31] Despite the confusion and hostility which greeted the idea of competence standards, work began on trying to make them the basis for nationally recognised management qualifications.

As with all the initiatives in the past, from the commerce degree in the late 1890s, the diplomas in industrial administration and business administration in the inter-war years, and the DMS and

MBA in the 1960s, there is an expectation that demand from employers will follow supply. But none of these earlier qualifications had aroused the expected demand, and there is little indication that further initiatives to certificate managers will fare any better. Recent surveys have shown that, as in the 1890s, innate ability and job experience are seen as the most important determinants of an effective manager.[32] This view is also shared by employers in Germany, Japan and the USA, but in these countries it is more widely accepted that innate ability and job experience can be affected by education and training. All three countries have in common a strong belief in education and training as an investment, and a belief by the corporations in the importance of their managers. British industry has also characteristically adopted a short-term approach to management formation. Its interest has closely followed short-term fluctuations in the business environment. It has not trained for stock. This short-termism has meant that new initiatives in the education system have not been given time to develop and adjust before business support has been withdrawn. Firms have not been attracted to comprehensive schemes of in-company training, whose results are of necessity longer-term.

The large corporations have made the most efforts to educate and train managers. They have had more need to attract and retain better quality recruits, and they have had the finances to train them in an increasingly systematic way. Programmes of management training have also usually depended on the interest of someone, or some group, in top management in these large firms for their beginning and continuance. Thus, it seems clear that an increase in the number of people in top management with an interest in management training would be a more certain way of raising the overall level of activity than further new offerings of formal qualifications. There is also evidence that top managers who are themselves educated and trained 'both encourage their subordinates to do likewise and seek high levels of continuing retraining for themselves'.[33] The problem is how to increase the number of people in top posts who have themselves experienced education and training.

Since the late 1980s the necessity for some inroad into the high level of voluntarism so long enjoyed by British employers in the area of education and training has become more acceptable. *The*

161

Independent, for example, has argued that there is only one way to begin to address the problem of skill shortages. 'It is to make it an offence for employers to recruit anyone under the age of eighteen without providing systematic training leading to recognised vocational qualifications.'[34] Towards the making of managers, Handy proposed statutory regulations which would compel companies to provide annual details of their training and development activities, and statutory subscriptions from companies to support a British equivalent of the German Chamber of Commerce, which does so much to assist smaller firms.[35] To these could be added, as a beginning, a requirement for all new full-time directors in public companies to have undergone a course of training, such as is run by the Institute of Directors, to prepare them for boardroom duties. The men at the very top of British companies, the directors, are still themselves 'amateurs'. A survey in 1990 found that only one in ten had received any training for their job and less than a quarter had gained professional or management qualifications. Three-quarters of the respondents were company chairmen or the equivalent.[36] The focus of attention must move away from those who might be promoted towards those who are already in positions of power and able to institute change.

References

1 Education, Science and Arts Committee, *Fifth Report*, I, HMSO, 1980, p. 76.

2 D. F. Channon, *The Strategy and Structure of British Enterprise*, Macmillan, 1973, p. 71.

3 Channon, *Strategy and Structure*, p. 75.

4 M. Wheatcroft, *The Revolution in British Management Education*, Pitman, 1970, p. 90.

5 Wheatcroft, *The Revolution*, p. 99.

6 Wheatcroft, *The Revolution*, p. 54.

7 Wheatcroft, *The Revolution*, p. 142.

8 Management Education, Training and Development Committee, *Second Report*, NEDO, October 1971, p. 6.

9 Wheatcroft, *The Revolution*, p. 105.

10 NEDO, *Second Report*, p. 4.

11 D. S. Markwell and T. J. Roberts, *Organisation of Management Development Programmes*, Gower Press, 1969, p. 165.

12 Wheatcroft, *The Revolution*, p. 84.

13 NEDO, *Second Report*, p. 6.

14 Wheatcroft, *The Revolution*, p. 125.

15 NEDO, *Second Report*, p. 2.

16 H. Mintzberg, *The Nature of Managerial Work*, Harper and Row, New York, 1973, p. 3.

17 R. Stewart, *Contrasts in Management*, McGraw Hill, 1976, p. 125.

18 I. Glover, 'Professionalism and manufacturing industry', in M. Fores and I. Glover, eds., *Manufacturing and Management*, HMSO, 1976, p. 116.

19 P. G. Forrester, *The British MBA*, Cranfield Press, Cranfield, 1986, p. 7.

20 R. Whitley, A. Thomas and J. Marceau, *Masters of Business? Business Schools and Business Graduates in Britain and France*, Tavistock, 1981, p. 24.

21 A. Sorge, 'The management tradition: a continental view', in Fores and Glover, *Manufacturing and Management*, p. 101.

22 Sorge, 'The management tradition', p. 103.

23 P. Armstrong, 'The abandonment of productive intervention in management teaching syllabi', Warwick IR paper, 1987, p. 2.

24 Whitley *et al.*, *Masters of Business?*, p. 58.

25 C. Handy, C. Gordon, I. Gow and C. Randlesome, *Making Managers*, Pitman, 1988, p. 169.

26 C. Handy, *The Making of Managers*, NEDO, 1987, p.88.

27 Handy *et al.*, *Making Managers*, p. 173.

28 I. L. Mangham and M. S. Silver, *Management Training*, DTI Report, June 1986.

29 Handy, *The Making of Managers*, p. 11.

30 Handy *et al.*, *Making Managers*, p. 178.

31 *Modern Management*, IV, Winter 1990, p. 6.

32 J. Constable and R. McCormick, *The Making of British Managers*, BIM/CBI, 1987, p. 3.

33 Constable and McCormick, *The Making of British Managers*, p. 22.

34 *The Independent*, 6 June 1991, p. 26.

35 Handy, *The Making of Managers*, p. 19.

36 C. Coulson-Thomas, *Professional Development of and for The Board*, Institute of Directors, 1990, reported in *The Independent*, 20 February 1990.

Sources

British Association for Commercial and Industrial Education
Association for the Advancement of Education in Industry and Commerce Reports and Proceedings (including annual conferences) 1920–30; Executive Committee Minute Books 1931–36, published Journal and Reports.

British Institute of Management
Institute of Industrial Administration *Journal* 1921–22, 1941–46, Council Minutes 1948–49, 1955–56, Education Committee Minutes 1951–52.
Management Research Groups 2 – 8 Council Meeting Minutes 1934–38, 1940–61, Annual General Meetings 1934–56, unpublished reports.

ICI
Files: Staff Recruitment and Training 1926–47 Box 274, Public School Boys MP 1926–32 Box 328, Scientific Training 1926–29 Box 457; Central Administration Committee supporting papers.

John Lewis Partnership
The *Gazette* 1918–60, various separate papers on the learnership scheme.

London School of Economics and Political Science
Management Research Group 1 (Ward Papers) Files: Labour Section 1929–34, Selling Section 1928–38, Purchasing Section 1929–34, Directors' Dinners Discussions 1931–47, Executive Committee Minutes 1929–58; Bulletins 1931–57.
LSE Files: Court of Governors and Council of Management 1929–32, Emergency Committee 1922–27, 1929–30, Professorial Council

1931–38, University of London Commerce Degree Bureau 1934–37 and Appointments Board, Commerce Committee 1924–28 and Sub-Committee 1931, Department of Business Administration 1928–57, Press Cuttings 1895–1924, Commerce Degree Press Cuttings; Advisory Committee on Railway Subjects and Minute Books 1915–38.

University of Birmingham
Appointments Board Annual Reports 1932–40, 1947–70; Reports of the Dean of the Faculty of Commerce 1902–16, Minutes of the Faculty of Commerce 1902–39; Reports of the Principal to the Council 1900–53; Books of Press Cuttings.

University of Cambridge
Appointments Board Annual Reports of Men's Board 1899–1976, Reports on Visits to Employers 1920–59, Special Enquiry into University Education and Business 1932–46; Women's Appointments Board Minutes 1930–39.

University of London
Appointments Board Annual Reports in Senate Minute Books 1916–51.

University of Manchester
Minute Books of the Faculty of Commerce 1903–53; Minute Books of the Proceedings of Senate 1903–28; Reports of the Council to the Court of Governors 1904–61 (includes Annual Reports of Appointments Board 1918–21); Appointments Board Annual Reports 1935–51 and Council Minutes.

University of Manchester Institute of Science and Technology
Manchester College of Technology's Department of Industrial Administration Minute Books of Advisory Committee (including Director's Reports) 1918–56, staff files 1919–41.

University of Warwick Modern Records Centre
The Federation of British Industries Bulletin 1917–21, Education Committee Minutes 1918–49, Annual Reports 1925–31.

Index